Praise for *Finding Equilibrium*

'Diving into a great leadership book is akin to a heart-to-heart with a mentor who's seen it all. That's exactly what it's like to step into the pages of Tanya's latest book, *Finding Equilibrium*.

This isn't your run-of-the-mill leadership manual, it's a personal conversation, especially for those of us who lead with thoughtfulness and introspection. Tanya doesn't just share her journey; she lays out a path that's relatable and attainable for even the most reserved among us. What really caught my attention though, was Tanya's knack for breaking down the complex world of leadership into bite-sized, manageable pieces.

Wherever you stand on your leadership path, Tanya's insights on improving mental wellness at work, striking a leadership balance and breaking free from the chains of workaholism are downright inspiring. And, I might add, so needed right now.

Finding Equilibrium shines as a guiding light for anyone yearning to lead with a mix of empathy, equilibrium and a solid commitment to the mental and emotional health of their team. Tanya's storytelling is vivid, her advice pragmatic. It's a book for leaders who aim to create a work environment that's not only productive but also positive and inclusive.

This book goes beyond mere information; it's transformational.'

–Emma McQueen, business coach, host of *Tea with the Queen* podcast, author of *Go-getter*

'If you are committed to mentally healthy workplaces, you need *Finding Equilibrium*, a guide to finding better work-life balance. This book provides the right balance of research and models to develop an evidence-based case for change in your workplace. The case studies tell the stories we have all experienced.

Whether you are looking to make changes to your own work patterns, help someone else make changes for a healthier better version of themselves or help teams think and work differently, *Finding Equilibrium* can set you on the right path.

The practical advice on how to support different leadership styles has given me lots of strategies and tools to help leaders in my workplace. This book needed to be written. Thank you, Tanya, for making that happen.'

–Debbie Fankhauser, people & customer executive, CPHR

'*Finding Equilibrium* is a comprehensive toolkit for modern leaders. In a world of relentless change, increasing demands and mounting pressure, this book provides practical strategies and research-backed insights to help leaders lead themselves and their teams sustainably, safely and effectively. Tanya's guide equips you with the tools to maintain balance, prevent burnout and drive success. I have no doubt it will help a lot of people, just as it helped me.'

–Leah Mether, communication and soft skill specialist,
author of *Steer Through the Storm* and *Soft is the New Hard*

'Living true to the concept of equilibrium, reading this book provided me with a beautiful balance of intellectual synthesis of extensive research through to lived human experiences in real workplaces. I laughed out loud at Tanya's clever one liners from bug zappers to exploding porridge!

It's a gift to be able to make sense of complex workplace issues in relatable ways. Thank you, Tanya for generously sharing who you are – it is felt and experienced on every page. Your passionate work enables us to explore how we continue to step into leadership and find equilibrium for ourselves, each other and our organisations.'

–Veronica Haslam, leadership transformation coach

'I want to take a moment to share that I continue to be impressed and proud of you, to work with you and share a deep and respectful mother/daughter bond. This book is fabulous and so practical. You have done an amazing job of sharing your theoretical knowledge so your readers easily find solutions or suggestions they can apply straight away.

Finding Equilibrium is a modern leader's handbook. Knowing that you have lived experience of the issues you talk about is so powerful for readers. I know that leaders at all levels will find value here. It is relevant, informative and visually impressive, without complex jargon or confusing language. I loved it.'

–Alexandra Heaney, associate consultant, chief of cheer squad, wise daughter

'In *Finding Equilibrium*, Tanya draws on her wealth of knowledge of human resources and leadership to provide leaders with practical and insightful guidance. As always, Tanya shares generously and often vulnerably, which beautifully enriches the learnings. This is a fabulous resource for leaders in the fast-paced, demanding world of work.'

Georgie Chapman, partner, HR Legal

Finding Equilibrium

FINDING EQUILIBRIUM

How to Lead Safely and Effectively in the Modern World of Work

TANYA HEANEY-VOOGT

Published by Tanya Heaney-Voogt
First published in 2024 in Melbourne, Australia
Copyright © Tanya Heaney-Voogt
tanyaheaneyvoogt.com
Melbourne, Victoria

This book uses stories to enforce the meaning behind relevant chapters. Permission to use these stories has been provided.

Every effort has been made to trace (and seek permission for the use of) the original source of material used within this book. Where the attempt has been unsuccessful, the publisher would be pleased to hear from the author or publisher to rectify any omission.

Edited by Jenny Magee
Cover design by Alexandra Heaney
Designed, typeset and printed in Australia by BookPOD

ISBN: 978-0-6455002-2-6 (pbk) ISBN: 978-0-6455002-3-3 (ebook)

NATIONAL LIBRARY OF AUSTRALIA

A catalogue record for this book is available from the National Library of Australia

Acknowledgements

Mr V. Twenty years with you has been a blessing. You so tirelessly accept my constant squirrelling and rabbit hole moments (and there are many) and rarely murmur about the hours of alone time I need to ideate, plan and write a book. You are neglected but so very much loved, and thankfully, you are gracious enough to only talk about the latter.

To my team: thank you, for collating and formatting those lengthy references, the sense checking, the feedback on my whiteboard mind mapping, the supporting research activities and your constant support and belief in the work we do. Special thanks to Alexandra for designing the Finding Equilibrium model and for your wonderful book cover. Your graphic design skills are exceptional!

To the amazing humans I get to work with who are committed to finding equilibrium in their own leadership and their workplace. Your transformational leadership inspires me and I could not be more grateful to work with you on your change journey.

To my generous early readers – thank you so much for your time and effort in helping to make this book even better.

My editor, Jenny Magee. Jen, this one was a biggy. It was a joy to partner with you again and I can't thank you enough for the TLC you showed to baby number two.

Sylvie Blair at BookPOD, you are nothing short of remarkable. Thank you again for making the book design, production and collateral provision so seamless and efficient.

Finally, when you say yes to something like writing a book, you say no to many other things. Time with family, with friends and the usual extra attention you pay to the people in your world. You simply can not do it all and throughout this book you will see how I have learnt this lesson the hard way during my career. So my final thanks are to all in my life who have had the 'rest of me' not the best of me, particularly in the final months of producing this book. I am so very grateful for your love, understanding and constant belief in me and my work.

Contents

Part Four: Getting the Work Done

Equilibrium

In the world of economics, equilibrium refers to the point where supply and demand are perfectly balanced.

The supply of goods and services meets the requirements of those who demand them.

When demand exceeds supply, the market responds accordingly and lifts prices of goods and services to reduce demand.

When supply exceeds demand, organisational profits may be eroded and waste occurs as prices decrease to encourage consumption.

Equilibrium is the state between those two seemingly opposing forces – supply and demand.

In the context of this book, those two forces are organisational outcomes (performance) and psychological wellbeing (of self and team).

Foreword

'You can't use an old map to explore a new world.'
– Albert Einstein.

'How are we supposed to do our jobs like this? We don't know what we can say, or what we can't. We get accused of bullying or told we're impacting someone's mental health just by asking them to do their job.'

Felice was exasperated. *'There's so much focus on employee mental wellbeing, but who's looking after us?'*

I'd been working with Felice as an external coach, supporting her efforts to lead a departmental culture change in a complex work environment. Many situational factors hampered her efforts and the pressure was taking its toll on her and others in the organisation.

That moment was the catalyst for this book.

Something shifted in me when Felice asked, 'Who's looking after us?' – because she was right.

Who is looking after the leaders?

Who is helping them find equilibrium in this shifting world of work? To navigate the seemingly opposing forces of getting the work done and maximising individual mental wellbeing (their own and their team).

Quite simply, we aren't.

This book serves to remedy that.

The Evolution of Work

*'We are attempting to find ways to ... redesign ...
organisations to make them more psychosocially humane
than those upon which our economy is now based.'*
– Robert Karasek and Tores Theorell[1]

Summer, Australia, 1982

I'm lathered in coconut reef oil, sun-baking and enjoying summer with my friend, Jen.

Our colourful beach towels with their white fringed edges are spread out in the back yard, just behind the tin shed positioned directly under the full force of the hot sun. The tin is reflecting the sun even more. We're smiling. Our tans are going to be superb.

It's 38 degrees Celsius.

We did the same thing yesterday.

It's exciting when we start seeing our skin turn red; we know our tans are developing.

We have the body lotion ready for tonight when skin will be stinging, and we'll take that hot shower and pour over the white vinegar because 'that helps bring out the sting' and moves us more quickly to the tanning stage.

We've got it down to a fine art.

If we run out of coconut reef oil, we'll just coat ourselves in baby oil.

I'm glad I can tan because I'm in the sun a lot. I'm a competitive swimmer. Every day I attend my swimming club in the outdoor pool, and every waking moment outside of school during summer I'm at the pool, sun-baking and swimming.

A real water baby. Life's good.

Summer, Australia, 2024

As a kid, summer was the best. Lazy days at the pool under the blazing hot midday sun. No shade. No sunscreen. It was just the way it was back then. We didn't know any better.

> *'Australia has one of the highest rates of skin cancer in the world, with about 2000 deaths per year as a result of the disease.'* [2]

We learnt the hard way and then shared those learnings with others to avoid the same poor outcomes.

And that's made a difference with research showing that *'environmental and behavioural changes achieved since the 1980s have likely contributed to the decline in younger Australians – the cohort who have had the benefit of skin cancer prevention programs for most of their lives.'* [3]

I can't help but make correlations with leadership. How we managed work in the 1980s was as potentially impactful as how we fried ourselves like sausages under the sun.

Now we know to Slip, Slop, Slap, Seek and Slide (two new additions). We also know what helps keep workers physically and psychologically safe.

Much like our sun-baking days, some of us look back on those earlier leadership behaviours with some horror.

Yet we learn.

Life is not static; things evolve, reveal themselves and change.

And we learn.

We take these new developments and revelations and determine new ways of working that we know will help people be productive, creative, engaged, healthy and happy at work.

Change is not linear and we don't all reach the same destination at the same time. That means there may be topics or musings within this book that challenge you. Much like the SunSmart campaign of the 1980s did for the sun-loving Australian population.

If you feel that nudge of resistance, stay with it. You may be breaking through a comfort zone, a self-limiting belief, or an unconscious or conscious bias. Or you may just be discovering something new. After all, learning can be uncomfortable.

Finding equilibrium will require you to push through those mental barriers.

You may not initially understand the rationale behind psychological safety, psychosocial hazards, job redesign, motivation, engagement, job resources and demands, and that's okay. We didn't really understand the Slip, Slop, Slap campaign at first, either.

But over time, you'll come to understand it. You'll see the 'why' and appreciate the positive changes that focusing on these elements can bring.

Industrial models of work

One of the most significant changes in the history of work came with the Industrial Revolution in the late 18th and early 19th centuries.

As new machinery was introduced, work shifted and became more industrialised. People moved from regional areas into city centres to work in factories. It essentially changed how they lived and worked. The resulting disastrous pollution, overcrowding, extreme poverty and social division gave an early glimpse of the law of unintended consequences.

The industrial model of work involved mass production, with assembly lines and repetitive work often in dangerous and unhealthy conditions. Cotton mills with fibres floating in the air ingested by workers. Fifteen-hour days and extremely low wages. Children as young as six worked in these conditions. The socioeconomic divide was huge, and workers could barely feed their families.

That model of work had good outcomes for business owners and the production of goods, but took a heavy toll on social and environmental impacts.

Command control leadership was a key trait of the industrial model of work, with strict hierarchies, tight control, and rigid practices. Workers had little autonomy or control over their work. If they wished to keep their jobs (and therefore feed their families), they were required to obey orders and meet relentless production targets. In essence, workers were another cog in the production machine.

Over time, people began to demand better working conditions and higher wages.

Philosophical movements, such as the Enlightenment, introduced social change and human rights perspectives that influenced working conditions – particularly around child labour and long shift hours.

New Lanark in Scotland's south is a preserved industrial cotton mill and village that showcases the history of the industrial era and changes brought about by Robert Owen. An enlightened leader, Owen recognised the benefits of ensuring the physical health of workers, such as being well-fed and having shoes for their feet, on how they showed up and carried out their work. He also introduced a village school, medical care and a co-op to enable food to be purchased at discounted prices by workers and their families.

These models proved beneficial from a work output perspective and instigated further social change.

Author Elizabeth Gaskell published her famous novel *North and South* in 1855.[4] More than anything else I've read, this novel provides a compassionate insight into the seemingly opposing forces of mill owners and workers. It demonstrates how finding equilibrium – striking a balance between the two opposing forces rather than continuing friction and hardship – delivered a new model of working that improved worker wellbeing and performance.

Gaskell captures both perspectives so richly that you find yourself drawn to every character with deep empathy and understanding for their respective positions, even though you may not agree with their actions at times. In 2004, the BBC made *North and South* into a television series starring Richard Armitage.[5] The series and the novel are well worth seeking out.

Real actions, such as those from Robert Owen, and rich stories capturing the nuances of this challenging era, such as that of Elizabeth Gaskell, show that balance is achievable when there is positive intention.

Over time, new models of work arose, including the knowledge economy, where workers are now valued for their skills and knowledge rather than their ability to perform repetitive tasks.

The history of work provides rich insights we can learn from – if we are willing.

Lessons from the Industrial Revolution are as applicable today as they were then. While the emphasis has shifted from physical health to psychological health, there is still a need to respond to the changing needs of workers.

Modern workplaces bring new challenges and demands

Globalisation, the internet and the technological revolution have significantly impacted how and where we now work. Communication and information sharing are faster and more efficient than ever before. And that's another unintended consequence, given that they create constant distractions, impact our focus, add to our mental load and bring new psychological impacts such as cyber-bullying.

Flexible work-life balance, remote work options, paid time off, the right to disconnect, equity, diversity and inclusion and a growing emphasis on employee wellbeing are all now on the table. Add to that the fact that modern workplaces are multi-generational and change-saturated, with high work and compliance demands and teams that are often under-resourced and fatigued.

These factors, combined with a stronger focus on psychological health and safety across global workplaces, highlight the need to support leaders to navigate these conditions.

Supporting leaders to adapt to changing conditions

Studies show leaders are crying out for support to navigate this new era of work.

According to Gallup's 2024 Employee Engagement Strategies Checklist, only 48% of managers strongly agree

Leaders are crying out for support.

that they currently have the skills needed to be exceptional at their jobs.[6]

We need to build this capability to ensure the sustainability of organisations, maximise the psychological wellbeing of themselves and their employees and attract and retain a future workforce.

Leaders are between a rock and a hard place. It's not surprising, then, that they are more likely to be burned out and disengaged than their teams.[7]

Leaders need to feel empowered and given the skills and knowledge to understand the factors that influence their mental wellbeing and to monitor and maximise that of their workforce. At the same time, they must manage the increasing intensification of work to deliver on the expectations of the organisation and its stakeholders.

This is no small undertaking. A shift has occurred, and it will take time to realign, to understand and build the competencies you require to lead safely and effectively. And to find equilibrium.

The four parts of this book show you how to do so, through the Equilibrium model of leadership.

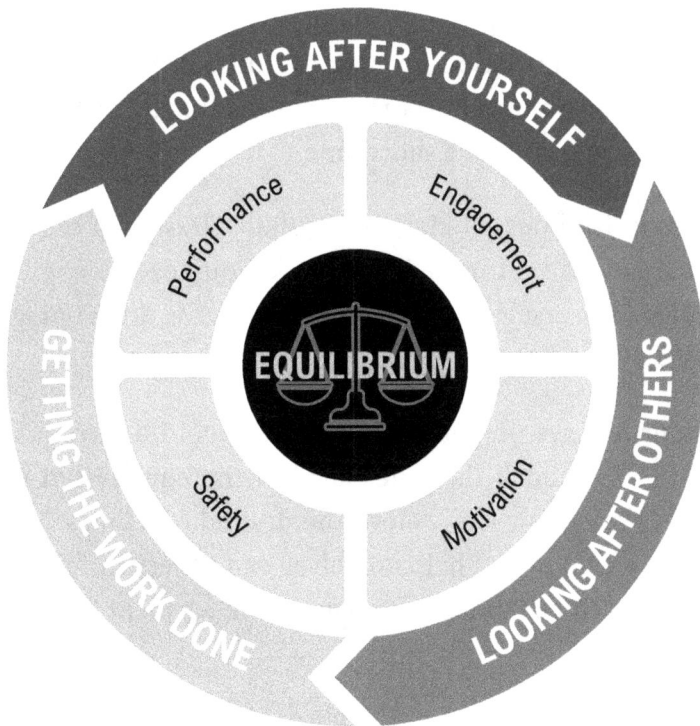

Figure 1: Equilibrium model of leadership

Part One examines safe and effective leadership. Here, I'll introduce my quadrant model, explore other types of leadership that may impact your ability to lead safely and effectively and provide insights for you to adapt or modify your style if required. At the end of Part One, you can take the safe and effective leadership assessment and create an action plan.

Parts Two, Three and Four explore the relationship between the three outer elements of the equilibrium model (Figure 1), remembering that none can be sacrificed for another. All three must work in harmony together.

Specifically, Part Two is all about looking after yourself and includes strategies based on high performance science to help you sustain maximum efforts and input. I want you to deliver your best for a long time, not a short time.

Part Three is about looking after others. Designed for leaders to bring out the best in their people. If you need to apply these strategies to yourself or manage them upwards, I encourage you to do so.

Part Four focuses on getting the work done. I'll introduce you to my PEMS model, the inner layer of the equilibrium model, which explores how we achieve the desired outcomes. How we get the work done and help ourselves and others thrive through a combined focus on performance, engagement, motivation and safety.

There's great information here to help you, the leader, understand the hidden forces that motivate and drive performance, help individuals be engaged and find meaning and stimulation in their work.

But most importantly, I will break down all the evidence and global knowledge and share the two golden threads of role clarity and leader support for you to focus on.

As Albert Einstein famously said, 'We can't explore a new world with an old map'. This book is your new map to leading safely and effectively in the modern world of work.

What this book is not

There is a clear and well-publicised link between physical and mental wellbeing.

If you are looking for guidance on boosting your physical health, this book is not the answer. I have assumed baseline knowledge and understanding of those principles and will let you get on with that yourself. There are people far more knowledgeable (and committed) in that space than me, so seek them out.

My focus has always been (and always will be) on workplace factors, workplace culture and developing balanced leaders.

While I won't be discussing nutrition, exercise, alcohol reduction or getting a good night's sleep, I will talk about why we often struggle to take action or follow through – even when we know something is good for us. To tap into that, we'll explore theories of motivation and the psychology of change.

Each chapter is as relevant to you personally as it is for your team. So share them. Learn, apply and model. What better way to lead?

Now that you know what you're in for, let's begin.

'The world of the nineties and beyond will not belong to managers or those who make the numbers dance... or those who are conversant with all the business and jargon we use to sound smart. The world will belong to passionate, driven leaders: people who not only have an enormous amount of energy but who can energise those whom they lead.'

– Jack Welch, Chairman, General
Electric 1981–2001

Part One

The Case for Safe and Effective Leaders

Safe and effective leadership is a core component of a mentally healthy workplace.

In my first book, *Transforming Norm: Leading the change to a mentally healthy workplace*, I shared the Wheel of Change model (Figure 2), which illustrates the integrated components required to build and sustain a mentally healthy workplace. That book addressed all but one of these elements thoroughly. Safe and effective leadership was always intended to be the focus of this, my second book.

I am delighted to now bring this to you in *Finding Equilibrium*.

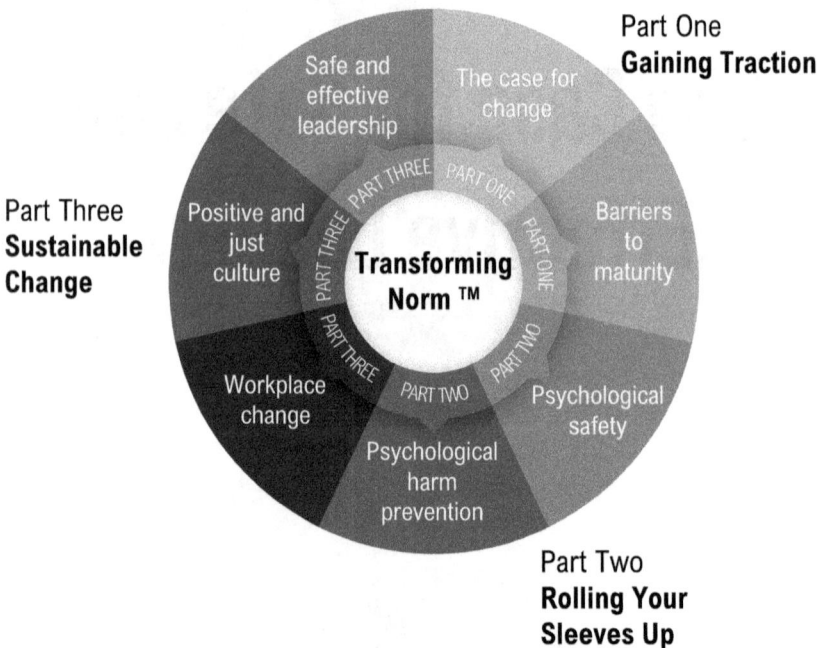

Figure 2: Transforming Norm wheel of change model

Chapter One

What Makes You a Leader?

'The most effective leaders are able to influence a broad group of people toward a goal, mission or objective. They lead. People follow. But rarely do we examine why people follow.'[8]

– Gallup

You are only a leader if others follow

In 2015, I was required to watch the film *The Motorcycle Diaries* when completing a master's level leadership unit.[9] I was not enthusiastic about having to sit through a film that I assumed was about motorbikes. The film is actually a screenplay based on the memoir of then-23-year-old Ernesto Guevara, who infamously became the Marxist guerrilla leader Che Guevara.

The film is an incredibly moving account of how Che's journey with his friend Alberto shaped his future activities. It portrays how the needs of the people he encountered – who later became his followers – deeply influenced his future leadership behaviours.

What makes someone follow a leader?

So, what makes people follow someone like Che Guevara? More specifically, what makes someone follow a leader in general? Global analytics and management consulting company Gallup set out to answer this question with a poll run between 2005-2008.

Frustrated by the focus on leadership studies in isolation from the followers that make them so, Gallup decided, 'If we want to know why people rally behind a leader, shouldn't we ask them?' The study sought the average person's opinion about leadership, through a random sample of more than 10,000.

In simplest terms, the research centred around two key aspects. Which leader has the most positive influence on your daily life? And what three words best describe what this person contributes to your life?

Synthesising the huge volume of information collected through the interviews, researchers identified that followers clearly understood what they wanted and needed from influential leaders. The researchers saw distinct patterns emerging from the 25 most commonly mentioned words. In some cases, more than 1000 people had listed the same word.

Gallup refers to these as Followers' Four Basic Needs.[10] They are trust, compassion, stability and hope.

While this research is nearing 20 years old, I feel these have stood the test of time. When I discuss these with participants in my leadership program, they concur.

Let's explore the four elements in more depth.

Trust

It's the bedrock of relationships. Trust is integral if you wish to engage your team.

Gallup's research found that the chances of employees being engaged at work when they do not trust the company's leaders are just 1 in 12. If they do trust, the chances of engagement are better than 1 in 2. That's a stark contrast.

A safe and effective leader builds trust through genuine collaboration, listening to concerns, demonstrating compassionate candour (direct with care), openness and transparency.

> Trust is integral if you wish to engage your team.

Compassion

Over many years of research, Gallup has amassed a mountain of evidence that positively supports the need for compassion in managers.

They asked more than 10 million people to respond to the statement: 'My supervisor or someone at work seems to care about me as a person'. Those who agreed were significantly more likely to stay with their organisation, have far more engaged customers, be substantially more productive and produce more profitability for the organisation.

Compassion is not the same as empathy. Compassion means you can objectively recognise someone else's pain and wish to find a way to relieve their suffering.

Compassion evokes action, which, for a safe and effective leader, could look like:

- actively listening to concerns

- identifying ways to alleviate intolerable job demands

- increasing social support or team camaraderie if someone is struggling at home or at work.

Can you be too compassionate?

Having too much compassion could put the outcomes at risk. For example, if you know someone is having a hard time at home and there's a firm deadline for completing a task, you may be conflicted. This is the reality for most safe and effective leaders.

If the deadline is absolutely non-negotiable, what can you do? Ask: 'What can I do to help you with that task completion?' Find the balance. If the home situation is really severe, look for another way to get the task completed. Be assertive and clear that the task needs to be completed while being open about how it gets done. Having said that, avoid taking on the task yourself!

Stability

In the workplace, nothing promotes stability quicker than transparency.

I often work with organisations undergoing significant change. As this can bring instability and uncertainty, one of the first things I encourage internal change leads to do is establish regular communication patterns. It's essential that they are never deviated from and that they contain responses to three statements.

> ▶ This is what we know.

> ▶ This is what we don't know.

> ▶ This is when we think/hope we'll know what we don't know.

Nothing promotes stability quicker than transparency.

This format applies even if you tell the same story every week or fortnight because you are still waiting on further information. Don't, however, set your communications any further than fortnightly apart. It's better to be repetitive than absent.

People will know that you will advise them as soon as there is a change. You have created trust and shown compassion for their situation, and you are providing stability through a consistent pattern of truth-telling. That means being open and honest about what you *don't* know.

Abraham Maslow's Hierarchy of Needs identifies safety as our second core need. In the workplace, this is essentially stability. Job security is the first place people go to whenever there is any mention of change. I see it time after time. Leaders must do what they can to provide stability, even when things are changing.

When ballet dancers first learn to pirouette, they are taught to focus on one point as a constant to avoid motion sickness. While everything else is spinning and changing, their focal point remains the same. You can provide this in the workplace through simple, regular, scheduled and consistent communications during change. If you can't do this broadly for the entire organisation, do it with your team. They'll still benefit.

Hope

'Nobody cares about the long term. In the long term we are all dead. We only care about the short term.' Those are my university economics professor's verbatim words when talking about the stock market. They didn't make much sense to me then, but as the years go by, I find them popping up repeatedly as I help create mentally healthy workplaces and future-fit cultures.

How do they relate to hope?

We're losing our ability to paint an optimistic future and give employees a sense of hope. Why? Because there's a risk that we don't have our eye on the long term.

CEOs and executives often have short (three-year) contracts. As a result, their focus is getting quick runs on the board to justify ongoing contracts or promotions or respond to KPIs. This is entirely understandable. We all need to show deliverables in our work.

Boards expect quick results from new CEOs, and external stakeholders expect quick results from everyone.

Politically aligned organisations work to election cycles and need good news stories to help win votes. Grant and publicly-funded entities need to prove outcomes to justify continued funding. Their focus is often on short-term quick fix activities that provide compelling evidence of effectiveness and demonstrate outcomes.

The problem is that most organisations have systemic issues that need rectifying to meet psychological health and safety expectations – and that work requires a long-term view and effort. If nobody cares about the long term, how can we create hope for employees that the broken things, like culture, chronic work-related stress and leadership effectiveness, will get better?

If hope is a basic need, how are we motivating and engaging our followers in the future state of the organisation?

> **If hope is a basic need, how are we motivating and engaging our followers.**

The situation is not good, but it's not quite as gloomy as it sounds. One of the other reasons we are more focused on short-term wins is that we are so used to reacting and less used to initiating. As work gets busier and resources become leaner, a survival mindset is creeping in where we just respond to what we must do on the day.

But safe and effective leaders don't shy away from initiating high-impact projects because they know these projects make success more achievable in the long run. Such projects are about organisational and human sustainability. Focusing on business growth, employee safety and employee engagement yields positive long-term results for the organisation.

Mix short-term wins with long-term, high-impact projects so you can deliver good news, quick win stories and create hope for the future.

Safe and effective leaders create good work

'Good work helps mental health and wellbeing. It can contribute to your daily activity. Your sense of purpose. Your income. And your social connection. But poor working conditions can harm your mental health and wellbeing.'

– BeyondBlue Australia.

Leadership has changed dramatically over the past decade, with more and more responsibility being loaded onto the shoulders of leaders. In particular, there is a heavy compliance burden and a growing focus on the people aspect of the role.

In many cases, there is still ambiguity about the role of leader versus manager – particularly in entry-level and middle-manager roles.

With so much pressure and responsibility to lead through the change, disruption and enhanced focus on psychological health and safety in workplaces, how are we supporting leaders to develop the necessary skills and knowledge?

Leadership programs rarely focus on providing the skills and knowledge for building psychological safety in teams, or understanding how to identify, assess and manage work-related stress risks.

We must support leaders to develop safe and effective leadership competencies.

In this context, safe means:

- ► being supportive
- ► ensuring clarity of roles and responsibilities

- remaining cognisant of and actively addressing work-related stress risks

- addressing poor behaviour or under or poor performance actively and within the parameters of reasonable management actions

- modelling and expecting appropriate behavioural standards

- providing growth and learning opportunities and safe stretch tasks

- having an understanding of job satisfiers and dissatisfiers.

Effective means:

- ensuring the work is done effectively and efficiently and that all deliverables are achieved

- recognising that the organisation exists for a reason and that each role fulfils a purpose

- working with the team to ensure these deliverables are achieved

- designing strengths-based tasks and projects for teams

- motivating and mobilising people to do the work to the best of their abilities

- fostering collaboration

- removing roadblocks

- leading teams through uncertainty and change.

Leading safely and effectively requires a focus on people and outcomes.

Leading safely and effectively requires a focus on people and outcomes. Finding equilibrium is the challenge of balancing these two seemingly opposing forces.

People versus task

The Safe and Effective Leadership Quadrant model (Figure 3) is designed for leaders in contemporary workplaces. In developing it, I considered model laws around psychological health and safety and contemporary research around work design. I also drew on the Blake and Mouton Leadership Grid, a model used extensively worldwide in organisational development.

The Leadership Grid is a model of managerial behaviour that was developed by management theorists Robert Blake and Jane Mouton in the 1960s. It was designed to explain how leaders help organisations reach their purposes through two factors: concern for production and concern for people.[11]

According to Blake and Mouton, leaders usually have dominant and backup styles. The dominant style is the innate, usual style and the backup style is the default when under pressure.

If you have completed a strengths or personality assessment, you will know your dominant style and possibly how this changes with stress. If you have not done such an assessment, reflect on a time when you were under pressure at work and assess how you responded. Did your usual style stay strong, or did you change how you did the work?

For example, a people-focused leader placed under pressure to meet KPIs may move towards command and control.

Safe and effective leaders simultaneously orient towards people and production. But they are much more than that. They have been supported into – or sought out – opportunities to develop their skills and knowledge to lead confidently in the modern world of work.

Chapter Two

Safe and Effective Leadership Archetypes

Understanding your defaults

Leaders have default preferences or styles. Knowing where you sit in the Safe and Effective Leadership Quadrant model will help you understand which competencies require focus.

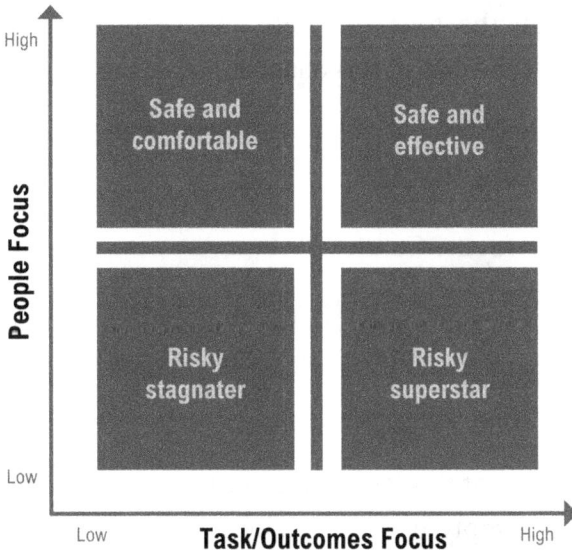

Figure 3: Safe and Effective Leadership Quadrant model.
© Tanya Heaney-Voogt 2023

Labels can be polarising.

I've included this model to enhance your self-awareness and provide activities to move the needle towards the safe and effective quadrant. A note of caution, though – labels can be polarising. This model is intended as a revealing exercise, not punitive. The purpose of this activity is for you to understand yourself in the context of work. Only through awareness can you create change.

Each box is a generalisation, so place your ratings anywhere within them or on the edges. Consider how situational factors impact your position. For example, when under pressure or dealing with a problematic staff member, do you move away from safe and effective towards the risky superstar quadrant? Do certain team members slip you towards safe and comfortable to avoid difficult performance conversations?

Read through the four elements and then complete the self-assessment at the end of this chapter.

The risky stagnater

Their natural focus: Comfort.

These leaders have been left in the shadows for too long. They're neither exceptional people leaders nor exceptional deliverers, but they do enough. Just enough.

They may have got this far by being unmotivated or underutilised, or they may simply have generally low drive or interest. Risky stagnaters tend to fly under the radar, but they are, to put it bluntly, an asset not delivering to its maximum specifications. We cannot afford them in our workplaces.

There are a few things we can explore to try and shift them out of this quadrant.

How to support them: Identify if this is a skill or will issue. Are there opportunities to explore other tasks that may re-energise them? Are they understimulated or underloaded? Do they need more challenge in their role?

Do they see the value or purpose of their role in the organisation? Do they receive feedback on their role?

Explore these questions, then coach them on behaviours and implement performance improvement plans if there is still no shift.

Here's an example of a risky stagnater.

Brent had been the department manager of a small team for several years. His reputation for laziness was well-known. The demands on Brent's division had increased tenfold, but much was not getting done due to Brent's lax style.

His team were frustrated, and it was common knowledge among his peers that nothing would get done if you went to Brent. As a result, people often went straight to his team, further increasing their workload.

Deadlines were not met and actions agreed in meetings were not done. There was always a ready excuse. One thing Brent was reliable at was absenteeism. Sick leave occurred so regularly that the team could almost schedule it.

Brent's new manager was frustrated. As a safe and effective leader, he was fair and relational – and focused on getting the work done. He'd established a good rapport with Brent and found him a likeable fellow. They got along well, and he'd felt comfortable checking in with Brent that everything was okay at home. He wanted to establish that nothing personal was impacting Brent's performance. He was reassured that everything was fine, just the usual challenges of kids and family life. By all accounts, Brent was happy and loved his job.

Yet, in terms of work outputs, Brent was not cutting the mustard, and despite weekly 1:1s and support and guidance from his new manager, nothing improved. Increasingly, it was identified that systems that should have been in place were not. But always there was an excuse. Brent's lack of energy and commitment to his role was not going to serve the organisation.

Brent and his manager met formally to discuss the list of projects. Those that were outstanding provided clear evidence of concerns about Brent's performance. Brent was given the opportunity to raise barriers or bottlenecks that were getting in the way of his success. Organisational barriers that could enable him to complete his tasks.

There were none. Brent simply had not 'got around to it'.

Having clarified that nothing was impeding progress, his manager was determined to hold Brent accountable. Was Brent demotivated in his role, which could be addressed with a little job crafting. Or was he just loafing? Stuck in a comfort zone.

Brent was a risky stagnater. He generally lacked intrinsic motivation and brought sub-optimal energy and commitment to his role. With no drive, there was no motivating force for Brent to change – until his new manager came along.

When we are low in intrinsic motivation, we need external motivators of accountability, consequences and drivers. Without these, we breed risky stagnaters.

You cannot afford these people. There is no room to carry the slack. They risk fueling resentment and conflict within the team as others experience a sense of comparative loss. These leaders impact team culture and, ultimately, team performance.

The risky superstar

Their natural focus: Outcomes at any cost.

Here we need the organisation's ethos to shift so the value is not placed on leaders who are ruthlessly focused on outcomes and less concerned about relationships and people. These individuals (also known as 'brilliant jerks') leave a trail of destruction and cynicism in organisations but are often promoted on the back of their technical brilliance or delivery of outcomes.

These leaders are high risk. They tend to drive people too hard and don't invite contributions or collaboration. They may see people as assets to be maximised. Risky superstars tend not to actively listen and instead punish mistakes and increase the risk of unsafe levels of work-related stress.

How to support them: Reinforce the need for *and* not *or*. Leadership is not people *or* outcomes – it is both.

Change organisational values to reinforce a positive, healthy workplace culture and safe working

> Leadership is not people or outcomes – it is both.

environment. Exit risky superstars who have no desire to change and can completely annihilate the culture.

Ensure their high risk behaviours are not rewarded with promotion and accolades. Coach them to understand the need for the dual focus and to become more people-centric.

The safe and comfortable leader

Their natural focus: People *before* outcomes.

People-focused leaders have highly loyal teams. Yet they are often predisposed to taking on too much due to their 'ruinous empathy' rather than overloading a team member. They can inadvertently miss opportunities to grow their people by solving their problems rather than coaching them towards accountability and responsibility.

Some people-focused leaders thrive on being needed and helping. Don't confuse this with servant leadership. Servant leaders clear the way for their team members to achieve organisational outcomes; this is a more paternalistic/maternalistic leadership style.

At their extreme, safe and comfortable leaders can appear indulgent and avoid delivering corrective feedback and monitoring or managing performance.

How to support them: Supporting these leaders can mean helping them build skills and confidence to deliver constructive feedback and ensure they develop team accountability and responsibility.

Discussing TED* (*The Empowerment Dynamic) and using a coaching approach may ensure these leaders aren't acting as rescuers.[12]

By way of explanation, the Drama Triangle is a social model of human interaction developed by psychiatrist Stephen B. Karpman in 1968.[13] It depicts three roles we move between as victim, persecutor and rescuer. These are generally deemed to be unhealthy relationship dynamics.

David Emerald later developed TED* (*The Empowerment Dynamic), described in his 2005 book *The Power of TED*.[14] The model reframes each of the unhelpful roles. As David Emerald says, it 'offers a new language; a new way of thinking – allowing us to create "healthy" relationship dynamics.'

Figure 4 contrasts the two frameworks. Creator is the positive, constructive alternative to Victim. Coach to Rescuer and Challenger to Persecutor.

Other ways to support these leaders include coaching to overcome the inner stories and interpersonal barriers that may make them uncomfortable about moving to the safe and effective zone, while ensuring they still lead from their values.

Understanding individual strengths profiles can create self-awareness. These are your innate, unique talents. We use the Clifton Strengths framework in our work. [15] It explains that our strengths energise us and put wind in our sails. Using our strengths at work engages and motivates us. However, strengths can hinder success if we are unaware and cannot manage their blind spots. For example, when individuals are high in compassion and people focus, this may stymie leadership effectiveness.

Using our strengths at work engages and motivates us.

Creator ▶ Focuses on vision and desired outcomes. Takes full responsibility for initiating action to achieve their desired outcomes.

Sparks learning by challenging assumptions and the status quo. Focuses on improvement and development by holding people accountable for taking action.

TED*

*The Empowerment Dynamic

Empower people through inquiry to help them gain clarity.

▲ **Challenger**

Coach ▲

Persecutor ▼

Dreaded Drama Triangle

(Karpman Drama Triangle)

Rescuer ▼

Thinks they must win at any cost. Controls others through blame, criticism, and oppression.

Intervenes on behalf of the Victim to save them from perceived harm. Fosters dependency by relieving the Victim of taking responsibility.

Thinks they are powerful and at the mercy of life circumstances. Is unwilling to take responsibility for what happens in their life.

◀ **Victim**

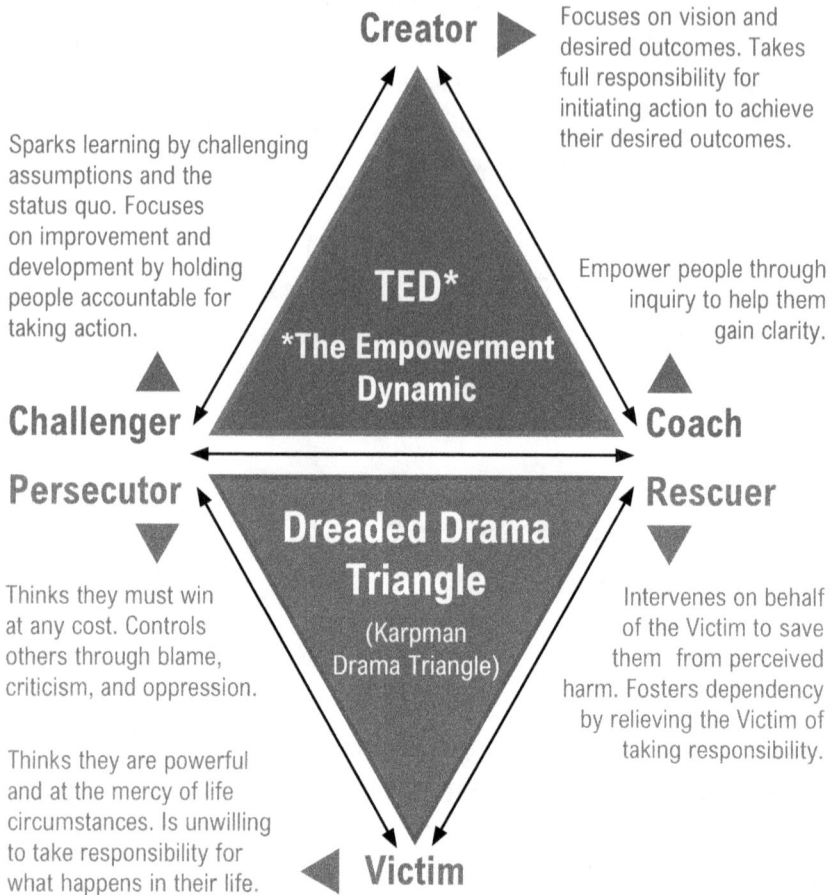

Figure 4: Adapted from Forbes 2018 article 'How to Escape the Dreaded Drama Triangle'.[16]

The safe and effective leader

Their natural focus: People *and* outcomes (interdependent).

These leaders enable their people to contribute ideas, learn safely and challenge the status quo appropriately. Their focus is on care and co-creation, not command and control.

Safe and effective leaders understand the laws of motivation, empowerment and psychological safety and bring out the best in their people. Their skill in providing appropriate feedback and corrective actions means they actively monitor and manage performance and promptly address any underperformance or poor behaviours. They face difficult conversations with humanity and openly listen to their people. They are trained in workplace psychosocial hazards (aspects of work that may negatively impact people's psychological wellbeing) and the impact of workplace factors on individual mental wellbeing. Psychosocial refers to the way social, cultural and environmental factors interact and influence our thinking and behaviour.

These leaders understand that the work environment is primary in enabling people to contribute their best selves. They actively strive for a safe working environment within the parameters of their control and influence.

How to support them: Provide skill development and coaching/ mentoring support. Reaffirm their practices and offer emotional support to have tough conversations if needed. Stay aware of psychosocial hazards and work-related stress risks and ensure they understand their role in monitoring wellbeing and organisational outputs without needing to counsel or diagnose.

Ensure these leaders have strong leadership support and receive recognition and reward for their role. Educate them on self-care strategies and ensure they have balance in their roles and appropriate recovery strategies.

The self-assessment

Understanding where you are now in the Quadrant model will help you identify areas for focus as we consider safe and effective leadership competencies. I've included the model here again, so you don't need to go back pages.

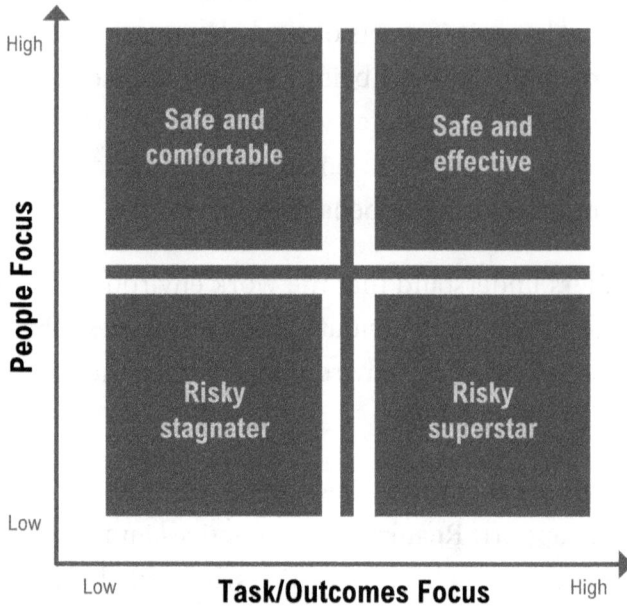

Self-assessment instructions

Thoroughly review each of the descriptors earlier in this chapter, then answer the following questions.

▸ Where would you rate yourself in this grid most of the time? Put an X on the grid (it's fine to land midway between quadrants) or describe in the space below where you sit.

- ▶ Are there occasions when you move out of the region you just marked X? When does this happen? For example: Which direction on the grid do you head when you are under pressure?

- ▶ What about when you have a difficult staff member?

- ▶ What if you feel your leader is not supportive?

- ▶ What other events cause you to move around the quadrants?

- ▶ Ask a trusted colleague to say honestly where they think you sit on the model most of the time. Where did they rate you?

- ▶ Do you agree with their rating? Did it align with yours? Was it better or worse than your self-assessment?

- ▶ Where would you like to be in the quadrant model, most of the time?'

- ▶ What gets in the way of you achieving this?

- ▶ What barriers do you foresee or currently experience that may impact your ability to be a safe and effective leader most? Be specific. For example, is it skill? A mindset? Confidence?

- ▶ What is one action you can take to reduce or remove those barriers?

- ▶ What would you include if you were writing your own development plan? (Refer to the suggestions under each quadrant descriptor for guidance.)

- ▶ Who could you share your findings and your development plan with? Sharing knowledge helps reinforce the learnings and will reaffirm your commitment to taking action.

'Sit in nature for 20 minutes a day. Unless you are busy, then you should sit for an hour.'

– Zen saying

Part Two

Looking After You

It can be tempting with so much work to do and people depending on you (your work team and your family) to avoid focusing on your own wellbeing.

'I skip breakfast, I prefer to get into work early while no one else is around and get some work done.'

'I'll take a break later, there's too much on right now.'

'My team needs me, that's why I keep my door open all day, every day.'

'I'll sacrifice my swim this morning so I can take Mum out for a cuppa. She needs some respite.'

'I don't have time to do a mindfulness activity or meditate.'

Sound familiar? I've heard or said all of these.

This section is about you. Because yes, leader, you do matter. I won't use clichés like you need to fit your own oxygen mask first. (I know, I slipped it in anyway because I still think it's a fabulous metaphor!)

I meet many self sacrificing leaders who do everything for everyone else first, and only do something for themselves if there's time left over.

As we learnt in the opening pages of this book, leaders are more likely to be burned out and disengaged than their team. Leaders often ignore early signs of stress, or fail to see unhealthy patterns of work commitment. (You'll read about workaholism in this section and take a quiz to see if this is an issue for you.)

This section is about you. How you can thrive at work and ensure you have energy left over for those you love.

Chapter Three

Sustainable Leadership

In a world of work where so much focus is on employee mental wellbeing it would be easy to believe that no one spares a thought for leaders.

Leaders are increasingly asked to carry the mantle of increasing compliance requirements, shield their teams from excessive work demands and carry the organisation's change efforts. In many cases, their stress increases as they receive little support to develop the skills and knowledge to do this confidently.

It's not surprising that burnout rates are growing.

WHO cares about sustainability?

The World Health Organization (WHO) is a big player in evidence-based sources of information. They call burnout a classifiable disease, although it's described as an organisational syndrome, not a medical condition.[17] While that last piece is neither here nor there, it does reinforce that this is about workplace rather than individual factors.

According to WHO, burnout is defined as: '...*a syndrome conceptualized as resulting from chronic workplace stress that has not been successfully managed. It is characterized by three dimensions: feelings of energy depletion or exhaustion, increased mental distance from one's job, or feelings of negativism or cynicism related to one's job and reduced professional efficacy. Burn-out refers specifically to phenomena in the occupational context and should not be applied to describe experiences in other areas of life.'*

At this point, I can hear Felice's voice ring out again. (Remember her from the introduction?) *'But who is looking after us?'*

Leaders absolutely matter. And this section is all about you and your sustainability.

You should care

Sustainability is a primary focus for many people, yet we generally refer to the environment when we hear or talk about it.

We only have one world – and we only have one you.

In this chapter, we'll look at ways to ensure your sustainability, to have the mental, emotional and physical energy to do everything you want and need – if, like most people, you need or want to earn a living.

Many of these strategies will build your internal resources, which research shows can buffer the more intolerable demands of your work and possibly prevent burnout.[18] More on this later.

You may find this section challenging and recognise that you need a mindset shift. However, if you are totally satisfied with your work/life balance, your health, your work performance and how you show up for those you love, then keep doing what you are doing.

If you've never had to take leave to recover, then you likely have strategies that work for you. That's great!

However, if that's not the case or you feel your strategies need some refinement, then this focus on specific workplace-based strategies is probably the most relevant section in this book for you. If you can't find solutions to bring out your best, boost your internal resources and buffer your job demands, then your ability to lead and bring out the best in others, including loved ones, and to achieve your personal and professional goals may be compromised.

And you deserve so much more than that.

Chapter Four

Know Yourself

'It's a marathon, not a sprint', said Kerry to Tori, a relatively new addition to her senior management team. Tori was perplexed. What does that mean? She pondered before replying, 'That's just my work pace. I'm just a get-stuff-done' sort of person.'

Tori was three months into the organisation and used to working at a fast pace. Her reputation spoke for itself when it came to her productivity.

Several years after this chat with her director, Tori told me she finally understood what Kerry meant that day. 'It didn't really resonate with me at the time,' she said, 'but now I understand. She was saying high performance needs to be sustainable. And she's right.'

Tori learned this lesson the hard way. As, perhaps, are you. As did I.

For most of my career, I've oscillated between two distinct styles: flat out or flat on the couch with nothing left in the tank. I run hard – until I don't. That's how I seemed to work and what I thought brought out my best. *'It's just the way I am,'* I told my CEO decades ago as I took my first two-week break, which I now know was related to burnout.

It's been a long personal journey to find my equilibrium.

Knowing yourself and your natural patterns and inclinations is crucial to developing sustainable work habits.

Over the years, I have incorporated many new strategies to sustain my high levels of output. That's because my personality traits, strengths and passion for work predispose me to over-commitment and burnout, and I have needed to make allowances for that.

All work has energising and draining aspects.

I also empower those around me to step in and drag me off the track now and then. My fabulous assistant, Alexandra, blocks out lunch breaks in my diary and dares me to remove them. She also notices when my energy is drained, alerting me to things I'm often unaware of.

The reality is that all work has energising and draining aspects, no matter how much we love what we do.

One of my programs is quite intensive as I work with teams that don't play well together to design a better future state culture. There's often a lot of negative energy in the room and it takes all my mental, emotional and often physical effort to get the team where they need to be.

After delivering a couple of these programs consecutively in one week, Alexandra said: *'You know, you're really flat when you come back from these workshops. I don't think you should do those so close together. What if we don't book more than one each fortnight?'* I checked in with how I was feeling, and she was right. I was drained.

Having people like Alexandra around you is gold. Taking their advice? That's priceless. We set up that little internal rule and adjusted our scheduling accordingly.

I've also identified that I can't function effectively if I fill every space in my diary. Check your diary. How much white space is there? Or is everything blocked out with back-to-back meetings? Protecting your diary and ensuring pockets of white space, or blocked-out focus time, should be a key priority. Guard this space ferociously.

> When did we stop seeing thinking time as part of our jobs?

If others have overwriting permissions in your diary, keep your boundaries strong. Explain why and decline any meetings slotted in your white space. This is your thinking time. Not every moment of work needs to be occupied by movement. Take time to think, consolidate and synthesise the day's events. When did we stop seeing thinking time as part of our jobs?

Early bird or evening lark

To find your zone of brilliance – when you are at your best to do deep, complex tasks, read Donna McGeorge's brilliant book *The First Two Hours*; it's a gamechanger.[19]

For me, the best time is always between 6 and 8 am. I'm rarely effective when I attempt to read research papers mid-afternoon. I can read 15 pages with no grasp of what I've just read. When I try again, I feel mentally exhausted and still have little retention or ability to synthesise the information. But at 6 am? Give me 15 minutes and I'm ready to share my insights with the world.

Knowing ourselves and when we do our best deep work is critical. The challenge is to carve out and protect that time. Let me be clear; this does not mean you are only capable of two hours of productivity – far from it. It's about identifying the types of work tasks in your day and knowing the best time to tackle them.

Not all tasks are created equal. Some you'll complete almost unconsciously, while others need all your brain power. Start noticing the differences and when you work on these best. When you've found your pattern, talk with those around you to set some parameters.

Collaboration or quiet

For as long as I can remember, I've needed quiet periods in my workday to do my best work. Those who know me well understand that I'm an absolute people person. I love humans and team camaraderie and the shared energy of a workplace, so it's not that I'm anti-social. Far from it. It's just that blocks of quiet time are an environmental need for me. And I'm not alone.

Introverted extrovert? Neurodivergent? Introverted thinker? Busy brain? However you label it, quiet is a visceral need for many people.

Radios blaring through the office? Ughh no.

Open plan office environments? Gawd no. (Research backs my view on this one!)

Chatty colleagues who go all day without drawing breath? Umm... Houston, we have a problem.

Play to your preferences

There are many ways to set up routines and systems that enable everyone to work to their strengths and reduce unnecessary stressors. Here are some I've seen working well.

- Establish a quiet time routine or quiet zone. For example, between 1-3pm we don't chat and we take calls away from the open plan area.

- Create breakout areas for focused work. To be fair, most well-thought-out open plan environments have these.

- Noise-cancelling headphones, with messaging on your desk to avoid the anti-social perception. I was talking with a researcher at a conference recently who said that when her university went open plan she put her earbuds in purely to alert people that she didn't want to be distracted. She was not listening to anything, it was a sign to 'Stay away, I'm thinking or in deep focus work'.

- Hold open and trusted communication with your colleagues about your – and their – needs and how you can find middle ground. Some compromise may be required!

- And, of course, use the working-from-home option on some days for focused work.

I need connection and I need periods of quiet. When those conditions are met, amazing things happen.

Surely, it's worth taking that little bit of time to find out what works best for you and your team to unleash all your brilliance. In doing so, you'll also reduce work stress and may even mitigate some team conflict.

Take a moment to consider what strategies have you seen or implemented that work well for quiet time in the work environment. What do you know about your personal working patterns, habits and styles? How are these working for you? And what areas might need changing?

Not all tasks are created equal

Look in your diary. Do all tasks require the same level of mental, emotional and physical energy?

Mental: Intense, deep or complex thinking.

Emotional: Relationships, dealing with difficult behaviour or emotionally demanding situations.

Physical: Long hours, physical demands of your job.

> Some things take little mental effort. Others, take all you've got.

Some things take little mental effort. Others, take all you've got. So support those tasks with downtime. I block out a lot of time in my Outlook calendar before and after face-to-face workshops, talks or seminars. That enables me to show up with maximum energy, deliver my best and have adequate recovery time to recharge my batteries.

Knowing myself as I do, I now intentionally and strategically design my week. Sometimes, though, I get an overinflated sense of my abilities and revert to the old ways just to see if something's changed. Maybe I can be Superwoman and deliver five workshops in a week after all. But no, I can't.

I need white space in my diary.

Energisers and drainers

How much of your work is truly fulfilling? There will always be tasks and activities that put wind in your sails and others that drag like an anchor. Plotting these can help you balance your schedule so you manage your energy.

Your working week

What picture would emerge of your working week? It's worth stepping back for a snapshot.

Make a list of the tasks and activities that bring you energy, and those that drain you. Can you remove or reduce any of the drainers? (e.g., what can you do if it's meeting overload?) If not, how might you adjust your schedule to better balance the energisers and drainers?

Which tasks do you find easy and mentally light? What heavier tasks require more concentration that you need to prepare for or need quiet time?

Do you consciously schedule those heavier tasks for when you are at your best? Or do you just fit them in when you can?

Knowing yourself and being strategic about planning and executing your work tasks and activities can boost your energy and job satisfaction and reduce the intolerable demands of your job. Set your intention and see where you can make simple and immediate changes.

Chapter Five

Master Your Role

You've likely heard someone say they've mastered their job, but what does mastery really mean? And how is it linked to job satisfaction and retention?

According to the Centre for Transformative Work Design, mastery is a component of good work design.[20] Good work design can transform a workplace to benefit the business, workers, clients and others in the supply chain. It can also protect workers from harm and improve worker health and wellbeing.[21]

> Good work design can transform a workplace to benefit the business, workers, clients and others in the supply chain.

We achieve high role mastery when we receive feedback and recognition from supervisors and peers and have opportunities to see a piece of work through from beginning to end.

Mastery has four elements.[22] Let's unpack these further and see how they work for you.

The four components of mastery

Feedback from the job

Feedback helps us to see that we are moving forward. Getting things done, making progress, achieving goals, staff progression – all indicate that you are on the right path.

Where do you get feedback from your job now?

What are two or three ways you get a sense of satisfaction from your work?

Feedback from others

Feedback is vital for development and performance. Constructive, corrective and complimentary feedback confirms that we are achieving what we should be.

Do you have people who tell you when you have done something well?

> Feedback is vital for development and performance.

Who reinforces that you are on the right path?

Can you check with others on how they see you progressing a task, project or problem?

Where can you ask for that feedback if it is not offered?

Role clarity

Role clarity means clear responsibilities, goals, expectations and priorities. It is much more than just having a current position description. Poor role clarity is a common psychosocial hazard.

Providing role clarity also means being clear about timelines and priorities when competing demands exist. Having role clarity provides staff with agency over their work, reduces anxiety about whether they should or shouldn't be performing a task and helps them get on with the job.

Is anything falling through the gaps? Are tensions rising between staff due to uncertainty over whose role it is to complete a task? Are staff struggling with competing demands and feeling overwhelmed, not knowing what they should focus on first?

If so, that's a sure sign there's a lack of role clarity lurking somewhere.

Do you and your team know which aspects of a broader project or program each person is responsible for?

Is everyone aware of your expectations in terms of quality and timelines? Have you checked this or have you just assumed?

Are you having conversations about changing priorities to ensure the right thing is being worked on at the right time?

Task identity

This element is often the least understood component of mastery. A high level of task identity means the ability to take a task from beginning to end. To achieve a sense of completion or reward for closing out a problem, a task, or a project.

> # When leaders are pulled between projects, task identity can suffer.

In change-saturated and high-demand work, task identity may be one to keep an eye on. When leaders are pulled between projects, task identity can suffer.

When that happens, people may lose the ability to gain satisfaction from completing tasks or projects. This can be demoralising – particularly for high achievers.

How well does your job allow high task identity?

Are you pulled from one task to another?

When can you last identify the completion of a large task from start to end?

Quick leadership tips for ensuring high mastery

Help people identify ways to get feedback from their role tasks.

Ensure you give feedback informally and regularly. Be intentional, and never assume (or believe) that someone doesn't need a pat on the back every now and again.

Be clear about role, responsibility, priority and agency expectations.

Avoid changing priorities too often at organisational, team and individual levels. Make sure you and your teams experience the joy and achievement of completing a piece of work. For large projects, break these down into tasks that can help provide that sense of achievement along the way.

Chapter Six

Workaholism

Are you a workaholic? No, seriously, are you?

It is not surprising that research has shown a strong correlation between workaholism and burnout.

For as long as I can remember, my siblings and I have referred to our father as a workaholic. His work ethic is relentless. Far more than just a strong commitment to his paid roles, he exhibits workaholic behaviour in general. He's always busy, always 'doing' something. Never at rest. It's no wonder his children inherited these traits.

One of the modern implications for those of us who have grown up seeing such behaviours commended, highly regarded and almost revered is that it becomes an ingrained belief and mindset. Normalised. Tied into our identity and often part of our unique value proposition when interviewing with new organisations.

When we proudly state, 'I'm renowned for my strong work ethic', we're really saying, 'I'm a workaholic' and bosses everywhere should clap their hands and jump up and down with glee. Shouldn't they?

No. Not really. Because research consistently proves a strong correlation between workaholism and burnout.

What exactly is workaholism?

Workaholism is generally described as an addiction. Researchers Andreasson, Griffiths, Pallesen and Sinha characterise it as being overly concerned about work, driven by an uncontrollable work motivation and putting so much energy and effort into work that it impairs private relationships, spare-time activities or health.[23]

> Research consistently proves a strong correlation between workaholism and burnout.

Essentially, workaholics are compulsive workers who struggle to limit the amount of time they spend on work despite negative consequences.[24]

Research continues on the root causes, but many believe workaholism stems from psychological factors, childhood influences, workplace factors (job demands) and a high need for achievement.

Other psychological reasons for workaholism include avoidance – redirecting our thinking into work to avoid uncomfortable emotions or problems. Sometimes, workaholics strive to gain approval and acceptance from others through high work delivery. And, in other cases, it's a maladaptive coping strategy of trying to meet high work demands by working more – even though such work investment is well beyond what is required to meet organisational demands.[25]

Fortunately, psychologists have developed screening tools to help us identify if our behaviours fit the criteria of workaholism.

While the Work Addiction Risk Test (WART) is the most well-known, researchers from Norway and the UK have developed a new instrument to measure work addiction.

The Bergen Work Addiction Scale

The Bergen Work Addiction Scale uses seven criteria to identify work addiction.[26] All items are scored as: (1) Never, (2) Rarely, (3) Sometimes, (4) Often, and (5) Always.

- ☐ You think of how you can free up more time to work.
- ☐ You spend much more time working than initially intended.
- ☐ You work in order to reduce feelings of guilt, anxiety, helplessness and depression.
- ☐ You have been told by others to cut down on work without listening to them.
- ☐ You become stressed if you are prohibited from working.
- ☐ You deprioritise hobbies, leisure activities, and exercise because of your work.
- ☐ You work so much that it has negatively influenced your health.

Professor Cecilie Schou Andreassen from the Faculty of Psychology at the University of Bergen (UiB) led the team that developed the instrument. Andreassen's study shows that scoring 'often' or 'always' on at least four of the seven items may suggest that you are a workaholic.

Does that sound like you or someone you know?

Seven steps to help a workaholic

1. Assess yourself: Take the Bergen Work Addiction Scale (or similar) self-diagnostic test to determine whether you may be a workaholic.

2. Check in with others: Ask family, peers and friends to see whether they feel you work too much or neglect other important aspects of your life as a result of your work commitment. Ask for their support, if needed, as you strive to make adjustments.

3. Examine your why: Go below the surface and examine why you may be experiencing workaholism. Try to identify what work provides you – other than an income. For example, is it perfectionism, higher self-esteem, status, avoidance, sense of achievement or satisfaction?

4. Know what you are saying no to: Consider carefully what is most important to you (income, status, relationships, wellbeing, meaning, family?) What are you compromising as a result of your workaholism? Is it creating strain in your relationships? Are you missing out on important life events? Given that there are finite hours in a day and week, identify where you could reclaim some balance if you are compromising on things that matter to you. This will help you change your habits.

5. Set limits: Restrict the number of hours per week or per day you will work. Limit how much you will work on weekends and your use of work-related devices. 'The right to disconnect' is a phrase we will be hearing more about and will see built into Fair Work principles.

While workaholics generally fuel their own behaviour, if you are engaging in workaholic behaviour to meet job demands, make sure you appreciate your right to disconnect and switch off outside work hours. That includes devices and your mind.

> What are you compromising as a result of your workaholism?

6. Check the physical signs of workaholism: Do you have stiff muscles, tension in your shoulders or jaw, tension headaches, back, neck or other musculoskeletal problems? Prolonged work – particularly in passive sitting jobs, increases your chances of adverse physical outcomes. Our bodies are designed to move and our brains need a break. Get up and take a walk.

7. Seek help: It's important to get professional help if you feel you need to. This can provide an understanding of what may be driving your workaholism and help address those underlying issues.

Chapter Seven

How to Thrive at Work

In this chapter, I want to introduce you to seven evidence-based strategies that will help you thrive at work every day. These include:

1. Recognise that mental wellbeing exists on a continuum.

2. Direct your energy to what you can control and influence.

3. Avoid bright shiny object syndrome.

4. FOCUS

5. Manage your mental load.

6. Avoid procrastination.

7. Inject fun, laughter and play.

These strategies are from my *Seven Strategies to Help You Thrive At Work* workshop and are outlined below. Combined with earlier guidance on sustainable leadership, make up this section on leading yourself.

Recognise that mental wellbeing exists on a continuum

Much like physical wellbeing, mental wellbeing is not static. It's like a speedometer, with green at the low speed, orange at mid speed and red at high speed, going up and down in response to life events.

At the green end of the speedo, we are healthy and thriving. We cope fine and perform necessary daily tasks while experiencing the usual ebb and flow of moods.

As the speedo starts to climb, we start to notice prolonged poor moods or distressing emotions. We may feel irritable and overly nervous, unable to cope normally, more anxious during the day or have trouble sleeping. This is generally known as the reactive state.

If the speedo climbs higher into the red zone, we start to experience distressing symptoms that impact our ability to perform everyday functions. We are no longer coping with day-to-day life.

A myriad of models represent these states or phases, from simple models to more complex wellness-illness continuum models and various iterations. Figure 5 shows the straightforward model used by Australia's national work health and safety and workers' compensation entity, Comcare.[27]

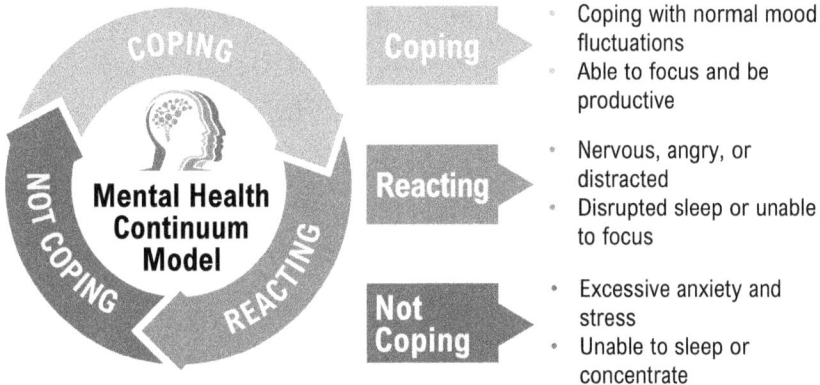

Figure 5: Mental health continuum model, Comcare

The key point is that wellbeing fluctuates and is impacted by stress, loss and grief. It is a natural and normal part of the human condition. Over time, when forces no longer take us out of the coping zone, we can generally return to normal healthy functioning levels of wellbeing.

For some people, diagnosed mental illness affects this continuum more acutely, and despite usual interventions, they may be unable to return to the green zone without psychological or biological interventions.

One in five Australian adults every year will experience a mental health condition such as anxiety, depression or substance use disorder.[28] Notwithstanding serious mental illness, people generally initiate interventions that bring them back to coping levels when they notice themselves slipping into reactive zones.

From a work perspective, work stressors add to our load and can move us out of the healthy functioning green zone.

Understanding how mental wellbeing works helps you to identify your patterns, your triggers and effective interventions – and may also enable you to better understand those you lead.

What about you? What pulls you out of the healthy green zone at work? And what strategies help to pull you back from the orange or red zones?

Direct your energy to what you can control and influence

We spend ridiculous amounts of mental and emotional energy worrying about things we cannot control.

In 1989, leadership guru Stephen Covey published his acclaimed book *The 7 Habits of Highly Successful People.*[29] The book included his model of influence and concern, with its two concentric circles. It illustrated the comparison between what we can do and influence and what we have no control over.

The variation of this model I use in training includes control, influence and concern (see Figure 5). Attribution is challenging due to the number of iterations to be found on the internet. But I trace the possible roots of this model to Neil Thompson and Sue Thompson's Control-Influence-Accept (CIA) in their book, *The Critically Reflective Practitioner.*[30]

The acronym CIA represents:

Control: Direct your time and energy towards the elements you can control. This will minimise feelings of overwhelm and frustration.

Influence: Be realistic about the concerns you can influence. Score your influence on a scale of 1-10. Move any concern scoring lower than 5 to 'Accept'.

Accept: These concerns are outside of your control and influence. Try to let them go and focus on what you can influence and control.

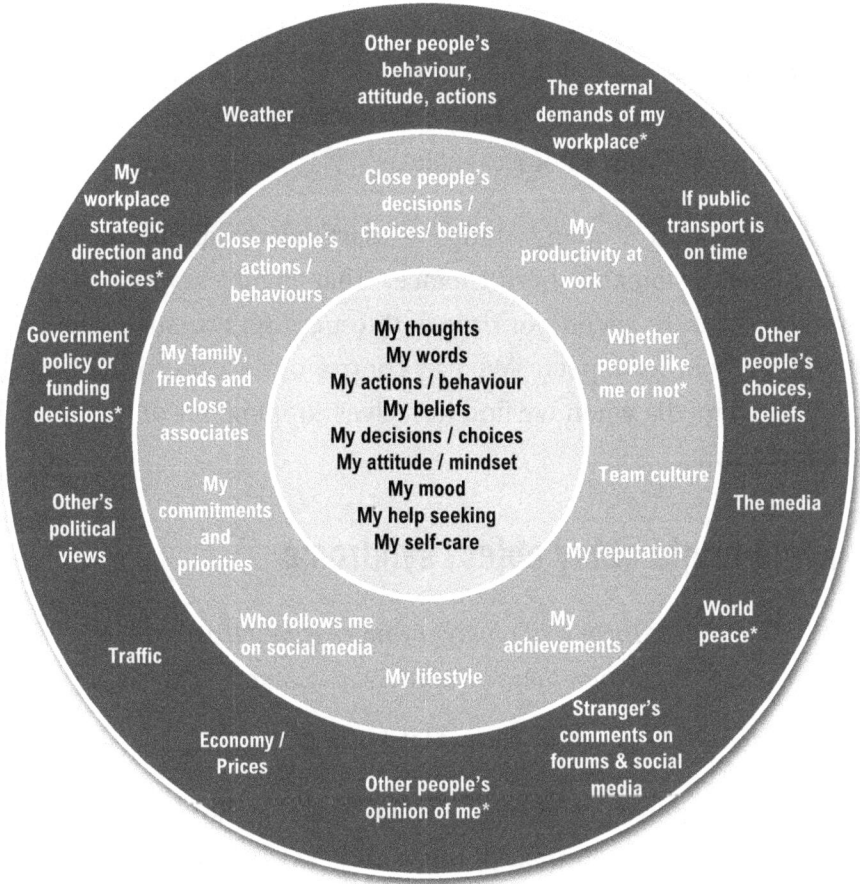

Figure 6: Control-Influence-Accept model, based on Thompson and Thompson 2008

(Note, items with an * in the model represent those items you may or may not be able to influence depending on your role within the organisation.)

Acceptance is vastly different from agreement.

If you have tried to influence a better outcome and cannot accept workplace behaviours or practices that impact your wellbeing and your ability to do your work, then you must consider your choices.

Acceptance is vastly different from agreement. We can often accept things we cannot agree with – as long as the cost to personal values is not too great. These are your decisions and yours alone to make.

We can control many things – particularly about ensuring personal sustainable performance. That involves what we say yes to, who we spend our time with (energisers versus drainers) and many other aspects. We can control our access to the news or social media when we find ourselves slipping out of the green coping zone.

Avoid bright shiny object syndrome

'There will always be more good ideas
than there is capacity to execute.'

– Chris McChesney

Does your brain catch ideas like a bug catcher at the summer BBQ? Is there a constant 'thunk, thunk, thunk'? Ugh, not another one.

There are always more good ideas than capacity to execute.

When asked how Apple picked a succession of winning products, Steve Jobs reportedly told Nike CEO Mike Parker, *'Focus means saying no to the hundred other good ideas.'*

We no longer have the luxury of focusing on one thing at a time, as we are sucked into the vortex of multi-tasking and copious distractions and demands. Phones ping, emails ping, LinkedIn and social media ping. People text, WhatsApp, MSN, FaceTime or Marco Polo us. All manifesting urgency and taking up precious mental space.

There are always more good ideas than capacity to execute.

The problem with these seemingly trivial distractions is that each is a note card systematically slotted into our mental filing system, labelled 'Must respond'. Our ability to focus is chipped away. This state is attributable to excessive demands or resource constraints and can also result from bright shiny object syndrome or BSOS. The risk for organisations that indulge in BSOS is that they do not remain aligned with their strategic goals.

Take Fred, for example.

Fred was a CEO whose organisation needed to do real work to ensure its financial and reputational sustainability. During a coaching call, Fred told me about a new telephone he was keen to test. He said the plan for the month ahead was to investigate and pilot the new system. His energy and enthusiasm for this task was palpable.

The problem was, that the goals identified at the beginning of our coaching contract were clearly organisational outcomes aligned to strategy and to remediating the known concerns.

Through our conversation, Fred recognised that the phone system was a BSO, a distraction. He had been caught up in the novelty and excitement rather than facing the hard work needed to move the organisation forward.

Of course, we need some fun in our work and ways to make the less exciting tasks more palatable (see later in this chapter), but not at the expense of core strategic and crisis needs. Watch for when BSOS gets in the way of success – individually or organisationally.

Less impactful events like this happen every day. Our busy brains are fueled by lives full of distractions. The power of getting the work done is in being able to focus.

Signs of BSOS

Here are some signs that you may, regularly or occasionally, suffer from BSOS.

Organisational signs include:

- ▶ deviation from strategic priorities
- ▶ yesterday's urgent must-do is no longer a priority
- ▶ not progressing or delivering strategic objectives within timelines
- ▶ resources directed to discretionary projects before non-discretionary work is completed.

The solution for organisations:

- ▶ ensure clarity on priorities at strategic alignment
- ▶ at peak times, focus on the must-haves, not the nice-to-haves

- create a central register for visibility over projects to monitor demands and resources

- remove before you add. Resist the temptation to add to the list, as each change dilutes the chances of success and risks change saturation.

Individual signs of BSOS:

- scattered thinking

- multiple things started but not completed

- inability to focus

- busy but not progressing or achieving.

FOCUS

Many people of a certain age know how important multi-tasking was – and yes, the past tense is intentional. It was high on the list of skills listed in our resumes and our cover letters proudly boasted of our abilities. It was akin to saying we had magical powers that few others did and you should hire us purely because of this fact.

I owned my ability to multi-task like a crown. And I don't mind telling you I was pretty smug about my superior abilities.

When high-performance researcher and author of *Strive*, Dr Adam Fraser, told me that multi-tasking is not possible, he burst my balloon.

Of course, having spent decades of my professional career priding myself on my ability to multi-task, I was initially

Multi-tasking is not possible.

resistant to this notion. At the time, I was working as a research assistant with Deakin University and Adam on a leadership wellbeing study. So, I did what any normal person would do. I set out to prove him wrong.

The very next morning, I was dancing about the kitchen in full multi-tasking mode, emailing and doing research work while cooking my porridge in the microwave. As I was demonstrating that Adam was wrong, I got my first taste of evidence to the contrary. Thirty minutes after resentfully wiping the porridge explosion out of every crevice of the microwave, I ate humble pie and 'fessed up to Adam that I'd seen the light. Some of us have to go down fighting.

The antidote for multi-tasking is to FOCUS.

Lynne Cazaly is an authority on new ways of thinking and working. She shared the acronym FOCUS with me when we worked together to plan my first book. It resonated so strongly that I have since shared it with hundreds of people.

FOCUS means **F**ollow **O**ne **C**ourse **U**ntil **S**uccessful

Brilliant.

Skating on thin ice

One of the main drains on leaders in the modern world of work is the need to be across so much superficially.

Very few senior leaders have the luxury of going deep, even on tasks they wish they could. We skate across the surface, but, as one director described, 'we feel like at any moment the ice is going to break and we will fall through'.

So while yes, technically, most people can do what they consider as multi-tasking, it comes at a cost.

Multi-tasking versus mono-tasking

Multi-tasking is switching between more than one task simultaneously. This has been proven to take more time than working on each task singularly and it eats up much more of our cognitive capacity.

Mono-tasking is working on one task at a time. **FOCUS** is the pièce de résistance, as it requires us to do just that. Follow **O**ne **C**ourse **U**ntil **S**uccessful. See a task through from start to finish without distraction or disruption.

> FOCUS is the pièce de résistance.

Manage your mental load

Your brain occupies around 2% of space in your body overall, yet uses 20% of total energy. Experts say your brain drains your energy 10 times more than muscle. So, while we might say the brain is a muscle – it's a hungry one.[31] Some researchers believe this ratio is fixed, so we can't fit more in, even when we need to. That is why it might feel like your brain is fried when you head home exhausted on those high demand days.

Ambulant workers or professions may think leaders just play on the computer all day, but these work tasks drain mental energy.

It's not just work tasks that call on these mental energy reserves. Interruptions, back-to-back meetings, competing priorities, emotional demands of tasks or relationship interactions (those challenging conversations that you spin your mental wheels over) all draw down energy. Or, more accurately, they add to your mental load.

In the 1960s, toy manufacturer Ohio Art Company launched a bright red plastic toy resembling a television screen.[32] It was called the Etch A Sketch, and it enabled children to draw patterns on a magnetic screen using knobs and or, later, other tools. Excitingly, screens could be erased instantly at the touch of a lever.

> Simple things like mindfulness or meditation clear your mental load.

I have fond memories of my Etch A Sketch, particularly the sound it made when erasing the mess I'd drawn. Evidently my Type-A ways were apparent even as a child, as the noise represented clarity and tidiness. I now use this wonderful toy in workshops to illustrate how simple things like mindfulness or meditation clear your mental load.

On a computer, opening an app takes working memory. If we continue to open apps without closing any and don't restart the computer now and then, the computer can crash.

Mental loading works a little like that. Each time we pick up a simultaneous task, respond to a notification, remember we need to pick up milk on the way home, buy a birthday present for Johnnie's best friend, make cupcakes for school tomorrow, or check that piece of data for the board report, we essentially open up a new tab in our brain.

If we keep adding without clearing some of this congestion, we experience mental overload. When we continue this way, we run the risk of mental exhaustion and, ultimately, breakdown. That's why we need to talk about it.

Common mental load scavengers

How many of these affect you?

- constant interruptions (people, messages, e-notifications, Slack, Teams, phone)
- back-to-back meetings with no white space in between (to breathe, process or prepare)
- push to multi-task to get through the work
- complex or emotionally demanding work or tasks
- competing demands and deadlines
- no time to reset
- peak work times that have turned into unhealthy, unsustainable norms.

The cost of interruptions

How long does it take to get back into the 'zone' after an interruption? By the zone, I mean that sense of flow, where you are productive and totally absorbed in the task at hand. Researchers at the University of California found it takes an average of 23 minutes and 15 seconds to return to your pre-interruption state.[33]

Do the maths. How many interruptions do you have per day? Take a guess:

Number of interruptions (nInt) __ x 23 minute 15 secs = __

Now divide that by 60 minutes to determine how many hours per day you are losing due to interruptions. Scary huh?

But we're told that good leaders have an open door policy, right? For decades, the message has been to be open and accessible. Even Timothy R Clark, author and creator of The 4 Stages of Psychological Safety, a framework in which I'm a certified trainer, says leaders need to be available and have an open door.[34]

How's that working out? If you are available to everyone every minute of the day, when do you get your work done? Oh, I know. After hours.

Let's try these techniques instead.

Four ways to preserve your cognitive capacity

1. Firm up your boundaries. Boundaries keep us safe.

2. Build white space into your diary.

3. Block out time between meetings and other focused work. Perhaps you could even eat your lunch then? Do not fill that space – and do not allow others who have access to your diary to overwrite it. Block out time and write DO NOT BOOK THIS SPACE.

4. Establish a protected/focus time routine.

This can be challenging for many leaders with a deeply held belief that they must have an open-door policy. While that's admirable, does it mean you must have the door open all the time?

Rafael was the principal of a large metropolitan primary school. Every day, a stream of students, parents, teachers and support staff entered his office for queries, guidance or just to let off steam. He prided himself on his open door policy.

But while everyone else's needs were being met, Rafael struggled to get his work done. It was normal to get home late, and his Sunday afternoon weekly preparation time was now starting on Sunday morning.

Rafael admitted that he was feeling exhausted, and, worse, his inability to catch up with work meant he was starting to doubt his abilities. He thought he was on the cusp of burnout and reached out for some coaching support.

I suggested that Rafael establish some protected time, where he closed his door to focus on his own work and ultimately reduce his time spent working out of hours.

Rafael was challenged by this notion. 'But I need to be there for people', he pleaded. 'They expect me to be available to them. I'm well known for my open door policy. I don't want my people to think I don't care about them.'

I reassured Rafael that I understood his concerns and responded: 'If you are available for your people 95% of the working week, do you think it is reasonable that you take just 5% for you as protected time?' Two hours in an average working week of 40 hours is 5%. Given

Rafael averaged closer to 60 hours, the actual time he struggled to take for himself was more like 3%.

Rafael exhaled. 'Well, when you put it like that, it doesn't seem much.'

'If, during those two hours, you write the school newsletter that you're now doing on Sunday mornings, you will regain two hours of family time.' His eyes lit up.

Starting small like this is the best way to establish a protected time routine, particularly if it feels challenging. Begin with one two-hour block per week, and build up from there if you find it works.

Establishing a successful protected time routine requires three things:

First, communicate in advance to those around you, what you are doing and why.

Second be clear under which conditions you can be interrupted.

Third, hold firm to your boundaries and don't sacrifice your protected time or allow others to disregard it.

Clear your mental Etch A Sketch

When your brain feels muddled, scattered, overloaded or fried, it's a sign you need to clear your mental Etch A Sketch.

It can take as little as three minutes to reset your mental load. Try some of these options:

Breathe: Three slow, deep inhales and exhales. If you know the box breathing technique, do that.

Do a mindfulness activity: My favourite is to closely examine a flower or a leaf. Watch a tree sway in the breeze or clouds floating in the sky.

Listen to a meditation app: The app Calm has a three-minute SOS meditation that is perfect! There are plenty of apps, including Smiling Minds, Insight Timer and Headspace. Find one that works for you.

> It can take as little as three minutes to reset your mental load.

Do one of these options for three minutes. That's all. What? You don't have three minutes? If you must go to the toilet to get space, here's a cautionary tale.

I once coached a leader on establishing protected time to clear her mental load. She resisted every suggestion, every strategy that had worked for others. There was always a reason why they would not work.

I suggested that surely she must get three minutes to herself if she went to the toilet. '*No*', she replied. '*They follow me in there.*'

This was a bigger issue than an overwhelming and overloaded job. It was poor boundaries and a lack of performance management. Short of a major disaster, there is absolutely no reason why a team member should follow you into the bathroom. If you're allowing that behaviour, it is absolutely on you.

You're reading this book because you want to find equilibrium. If you really want that, tighten your boundaries. Immediately.

Changing a habit is always hard, but there are only two choices when your existing work patterns are not serving you well. Continue your path to burnout, or try something new.

That's your menu. What's your order?

Avoid procrastination

Why do we procrastinate? For many leaders I work with it's a simple case of feeling overwhelmed with multiple competing deadlines, and not knowing which to tackle first.

Overwhelm fuels inertia.

This sense of overwhelm fuels inertia – and I'm no stranger to this feeling either. What works well for me are two techniques.

The first is that I have a master To Do list and pull only three things from that list each day. Chances are I'll complete more than three and grab another from the list, but looking at three items feels much more achievable than the dozens on my master list. Doing this daily also means I can adjust according to changing priorities.

I get my mindset right by deploying the **WDEP** model. This represents four coaching questions that extinguish procrastination.

W = What are you trying to achieve?

D = What are you currently doing about it?

E = How is that working out for you? Evaluate this.

P = With these insights, what's your plan of action.

I deployed WDEP many times in the final stages of this book. Here's what that looked like.

W = What are you trying to achieve? *Complete the final edits on my book.*

D = What are you doing about it currently? *Avoiding it and re-watching Season Six of The Crown on Netflix.*

E = How is that working out for you? *Well, a very loud nagging voice in my head is making me restless and spoiling my viewing.*

P = What's your plan of action. *Switches off Netflix, hits the computer.*

Trust me when I say that WDEP is a fabulous tool, and many I've shared it with agree. Try it!

Inject fun, laughter and play

In my opinion, this is one of the most underrated strategies in the workplace.

Mental: Laughter creates a chemical reaction in our bodies. It increases endorphins and serotonin (happy hormones) and lowers cortisol and adrenaline (stress hormones) to benefit our mental state overall.

Social: Fun, laughter and play increase connectedness, elevate mood, enhance positive communication, diffuse tension and relax us.

Physical: Within the first 10 seconds of laughter, 15 facial muscles contract and relax. Laughter stimulates the immune system, eases muscle tension and relaxes muscles in the face, chest and abdomen.

Laughter acts like a pressure release valve.

Laughter acts like a pressure release valve, letting off steam. Have you ever been with a group of people when you could 'cut the air with a knife'? Then someone says something funny and all the tension fizzles out.

What about forced laughter? Does that still have the same physiological benefits? It might surprise you to learn that it does. Activities like laughing yoga have the same benefits as unsolicited laughter. But be careful. Well-meaning efforts can backfire and create resentment where people are 'told' to attend laughing yoga, but work-related stressors aren't managed. It's far better to help people understand the benefits and encourage them to find their own ways to step into laughter rather than make it compulsory.

Appropriate humour is a non-negotiable. There is no room for demeaning humour or laughter at the expense of others in the workplace. (I'd say this is so in the world, but let's start with work.)

This brings me to a question that often arises when discussing workplace culture and team psychological safety – particularly around respect and civility. They say, 'Does this mean we can't have our usual banter as a team?' It is not uncommon for teams to have their own (more informal) ways of behaving that they consider appropriate and just innocent banter. However, if viewed objectively, these may appear outside the lines of appropriate workplace behaviour.

Usually the question is well meant. They say, 'We have a lot of fun, we know each other well and sometimes we sledge each other a little – or a lot'. I respond that intelligent humour is great; if it's crass or degrading humour, not so much.

I encourage people to be absolutely sure that everyone's okay with this vibe. Not just going along for the ride because it's safer to do so than speak up against it.

There is also a hard no on vitriol, sexual or discriminatory comments delivered under the guise of humour. 'I was only joking' isn't a defence.

> 'I was only joking' isn't a defence.

Play at work

Another way for individual play at work is to design your own game when performing those ever-present boring or draining tasks.

Professor Arnold Bakker is a burnout and work design researcher from the Netherlands. He describes ways people create a sense of fun that include using a creative word in boring meetings and keeping a daily tally of how many emails you can get through in an hour. Bakker cautions against competing against coworkers as play, as it can create tension.

I've seen teams band together and create playful moments out of crises. During the pandemic, a medical centre team created a game to see who received the most bizarre question each day. A customer service team in a local government agency did something similar after a local emergency event.

While this could be seen as cynical or disrespectful from the outside, this form of humour is a clever way for teams exposed to significant pressure and often high levels of customer aggression to release the pressure valve and buffer the more intolerable demands of their roles. It is in-house humour, a discreet team activity with the leader's involvement. In both cases, the teams reported that it created laughter and lightness during a really challenging period.

Another team used meme generators to circulate contextual memes via Teams Chat each Friday, assigning a prize for the best meme. (Clearly, you'd need some rules around this!) Other teams have virtual bingo or trivia. All to generate play in the day.

What makes you laugh?

Develop your own intervention plan and when your mood needs a boost, intentionally seek out things that make you laugh. These might include a funny television series or program, memes, or the antics of animals or children. British comedian Michael McIntyre is my go-to for a laugh!

If it works for you (and doesn't breach anyone's human rights or wellbeing), make it a core part of your plan.

Chapter Eight

Get In Sync With Your Elephant

Have you heard the story about the elephant and the rider?

In 2006, Jonathan Haidt, professor of ethical leadership at NYU's Stern School of Business, introduced the elephant and rider metaphor in his extraordinary book *The Happiness Hypothesis*.[35] Haidt takes us on a journey through ancient cultures and rituals and correlates these with modern leadership and psychological principles.

The metaphorical thread running through the ten elements in the book is the elephant and the rider.

The elephant represents our emotions, those unconscious, automatic and seemingly uncontrollable parts of ourselves that drive us to charge off on a path that may not be useful.

The rider is the more intelligent of the partnership. The rider is thoughtful, considerate, calm and not easily roused to action. It contemplates, assesses and weighs up information that appears along the path.

The elephant and the rider must work together to successfully navigate the path ahead.

Elephants and riders in sync

Why is your elephant so prone to charging off? Humans have a hardwired negativity bias that has kept us safe throughout the evolution of our species. It helps us respond quickly to perceived or actual threats, instinctively evaluating bad over good. As Haidt confirms, 'over and over again, psychologists find the human mind reacts to bad things more quickly, strongly and persistently than equivalent good things.'

We fight against this natural predilection to scan for and identify threats. No amount of reassurance from the rider will stop the elephant from seeing and reacting to a tiger. It's instinctive. There's a risk. Performance feedback, someone disagreeing with an idea or organisational change may appear as tigers for some people.

> Rather than controlling each other, the elephant and rider must work together.

While threat detection is a valuable tool, we don't always recognise when a threat is real.

When leaders understand how negativity bias plays out in themselves and their teams, they can work in sync with their elephants along a more constructive and thoughtful path.

Haidt is clear that despite the disproportionate power the elephant (automatic response) holds, the rider is essential. Rather than controlling each other, the elephant and rider must work together. Be in sync.

The rider can coach and support the elephant, and the elephant can help the rider identify things they may not see.

The chicken or the egg

Do thoughts trigger emotions, or do emotions cause thoughts?

Both can be true and perpetuate unhelpful judgements. When processing an object or event, brains go through a process of filtering known as mental heuristics. This mental shortcut-taking enables us to judge and respond more quickly.

When a real threat appears, mental heuristics can save your life. Here's how it plays out:

Event: Tiger enters the path.

Without mental heuristics: Oh, there's a tiger. Hello, pretty tiger. I wonder if you're a good tiger or a bad tiger. How could I find out? Maybe I'll just wait and see what happens.

With mental heuristics: Tiger! Tiger ate Bob last year. Tiger means death. Run.

These mental shortcuts are effective and necessary, but can reinforce or establish patterns of bias. For

> Mental shortcuts are effective and necessary, but can reinforce or establish patterns of bias.

example, if someone of a particular demographic causes you emotional pain on a random occasion, your brain may file this information away.

The next time someone from that same demographic acts in a way you construe as harmful, your brain scans the filing cabinet for evidence that this person causes pain. Your past experience means you assume the worst, regardless of the person's actual intentions.

Has that happened to you? Perhaps it was valid the first time, but it's not necessarily so on subsequent occasions. However, your mental filing system will keep recalling the negative response until you replace it with a more flexible view.

Rider to the rescue

Your inner elephant's job is to identify and alert you to threats. It's useful. Until it's not.

The rider's job is to find opportunities to gently help the elephant see past the emotional responses. To recognise that this particular tiger is not a threat, she's quietly minding her own business.

When the rider and elephant are in sync, the elephant isn't charging off in response to a mouse.

Are you up for an activity?

Imagine a picture of you and your elephant working together. What phrases could you use to strengthen the connection between you?

'Come on elephant, where are you heading?'

'Settle down, elephant, that's a mouse, not a tiger.'

'It's okay elephant, there's no threat to us.'

What happens when you fall off your elephant?

Things go wrong. We make mistakes. We lose our temper. We misjudge our communication. We err.

It's part of the human condition that we need to accept for ourselves and those we lead. Regardless of this, we punish ourselves and others for mishaps. Even with my passion for mentally healthy workplaces and my deep knowledge of safe and effective leadership behaviours, I sometimes fall off my elephant.

I was delivering a workshop and was repeatedly interrupted by a participant whose behaviour I found disrespectful. In hindsight (a wonderful thing) I can see that workplace factors had contributed significantly to their frustration and anger. But they were unleashing it on me – a third-party facilitator.

Despite my experience of speaking, facilitating and working with groups, their behaviour knocked me off my elephant. My elephant ran wild with no calming rider to redirect. The outcome was not as colourful as you might imagine, but I made it clear that I was annoyed by the behaviour. Essentially, I bit back, which did not align with my values or my personal standards.

There's no doubt that the participant was disrespectful and should have been checked by their leader, who was sitting two seats away. But I did not handle it well.

So, given my experience and expertise in facilitation, why did I react? Because I'm human. I'm subject to the usual range of human emotions and I am also triggered by certain personalities and approaches.

Some days, despite all efforts, the elephant dumps the rider, and no amount of emotional intelligence or self-regulation puts the rider back in the seat.

These moments offer rich learnings, once we've processed them and stopped beating ourselves up.

Not-so-intelligent failures

Intelligent failure is a failed experiment based on a sound hypothesis, such as a change to a hospital care model or an innovative operating model for an organisation. So says Amy Edmondson in her book, *Right Kind of Wrong*.[36]

But everyday individual failures? In my experience, they're rarely intelligent. Like my own mistake, there are ways to reframe these moments and reduce the associated shame.

Shame is a terrible emotion. It debilitates like no other emotion – except, perhaps, grief.

Why do we feel shame when we make a mistake? And even more so if we are criticised for it? It's because our vulnerability is punished. We are hurt and wounded. Our elephant wants to charge off and hide in the bush, convinced it's full of deficits and unlovable. If I could fix anything in this world, it would be the thoughts and feelings that arise from shame. It took three months to rid myself of the cloak of shame from the workshop episode.

Now, I feel something more rational. My rider and elephant are finally in sync about it.

Building mistake tolerance in your team is a feature of psychological safety. Sharing mistakes (and therefore vulnerability) is a key step. Normalising mistakes makes us human and strengthens connections with your team. Sharing your mistakes is surprisingly cathartic. If you want your people to learn and grow, openly table errors so they can be investigated objectively and steps taken to reduce their subsequent likelihood, then you have to make it safe to err.

> Normalising mistakes makes us human and strengthens connections.

Most high performers punish themselves more than anyone else ever could when they fall short of high personal expectations. Researcher Brené Brown describes perfectionism as a function of shame.[37] She says that we all experience the emotion of shame. Those who don't, lack the capacity for empathy and human connection.[38]

Brown's definition of shame comes from decades of research. It is 'the intensely painful feeling or experience of believing that we are flawed and therefore unworthy of love, belonging and connection.'

Move out of the shame cycle

Brown's research identified the following four steps to create shame resilience.

Recognise shame and understand its triggers. Can you physically recognise when you're experiencing shame and name it? Identify what messages and expectations triggered it.

Practice critical awareness. Can you reality-check the messages and expectations that are driving your shame? Are they realistic? Attainable? Are you holding yourself to a higher standard than you would your best friend, for example? Are they what you want to be, or what you think others need or want from you?

Reach out. Are you owning and sharing your story? We can't experience empathy if we're not connecting.

Speak about your shame. Are you talking about how you feel and asking for what you need when you feel shame? Silence, secrecy and judgement fuel shame.

As Brown confirms: 'Where perfectionism exists, shame is always lurking.'

Share your whoopsies

I start my leadership development program sessions with the three Ws. Everyone gets to share a Win, a Whoopsie and a piece of Wisdom (a learning). In the program evaluations, people always comment on the benefit of sharing Whoopsies.

Why? Because sharing them with our colleagues normalises errors and removes shame.

Reflect on your mistakes

Can you think of a time when you made a mistake? What happened? Do you still cringe at the memory? Have you ever told anyone about the event?

Talking about mistakes reduces the power of shame and normalises them if leaders demonstrate vulnerability by sharing their stories. That doesn't mean creating sloppy or negligent environments; it's about acknowledging the human condition that makes us fallible and providing rich learning opportunities.

A side note about elephants

I intentionally share Haidt's metaphor because of its deep influence on my journey to regulate my highly passionate and emotive inner self. The image I hold of the rider and the elephant is of deep support for each other. They are equals.

When I navigate my elephant, the rider is always gentle, loving and nurturing. It walks alongside, not abusing, beating or berating. In using this metaphor, I recognise that some real elephants suffer terrible cruelty and abuse. I do not wish to perpetuate or condone such behaviour.

Chapter Nine

Change = Knowledge + Intention + Action

We want to change, but...

We've all been there. You've read that great book or sat through that fabulous training workshop. You're energised, with Post-it notes bristling from every page and a journal full of notes.

You're committed. You're going to make a raft of changes, find equilibrium and revolutionise your life. Right?

If knowledge alone generated change, life would be pretty dull. There'd be nothing to strive for. So, why is it so hard to convert knowledge into action? It's a question many of us keep asking.

> Why is it so hard to convert knowledge into action?

Here are six reasons why we struggle to follow through on a decision to change.

We set the change gap too wide

Our current and future states are too far apart. The mountain ahead is daunting and we doubt our ability to succeed. We think it's too hard. (Remember Henry Ford's words. 'Whether you think you can or you think you can't, you're right.') We don't believe we can possibly achieve the outcome, which diminishes our performance because our efforts are only half-hearted.

That's why the first setback is seen as a sign that we should never have tried. It's not meant to be.

We fear loss more than we value gain

It's 5 am and your alarm goes off. Snoozing in a warm bed is far more appealing than starting that new fitness regime – even though you promised. I mean, sleep's important, right? And bed is oh so comfy. You can always start that new fitness regime to-morrow.

But of course, you don't.

This is a common example of where we fear the loss of comfort more than we value the gain from improved health and fitness. When I quote this example in my change workshops, nearly everyone nods.

We set the goal but don't create the systems to achieve it

The problem? 'We don't rise to the level of our goals, we fall to the level of our systems.' Wise words from James Clear, author of the international bestseller *Atomic Habits*.[39] As he says, 'winners and losers have the same goals'. That means the goal doesn't differentiate them. Systems of continuous small improvements are what achieve a different outcome.

Mea culpa

At the start of 2023, I designed a fabulous goals worksheet for my business planning and to share with my coaching clients.

> 'We don't rise to the level of our goals, we fall to the level of our systems.'

At the top were the three goals I wanted to achieve, and below were three columns. The left column included things I was going to do more of, the middle column was things I was going to carry forward and the right-hand column listed things I was going to do less of. All to ensure I could achieve my goals.

At the bottom of the template, I even left space for a motivating quote.

I reproduced my template in A3 size and pinned it to the office wall. It served as a great visual reminder of my three goals. I looked at them regularly throughout the year and stayed true to them. Although I admit there was less emphasis on what I wanted to do less of.

At the end of the year, my team and I reviewed the goals. I'd achieved two of the three, but only just, and it had been hard work and mentally draining. We had not worked efficiently, particularly in the last quarter of the year, which impacted achievement.

Why? Because I had not taken time to establish proper systems so my team could support me effectively.

We had grown the team and the business, but I'd essentially kept operating like a sole practitioner. I issued tasks as needed (or as I thought of them) to keep the team occupied. But, these highly capable individuals saw me working hard and wanted to help more than our existing systems allowed. They nagged me about taking time out to create systems, but I didn't recognise the value of doing so. Probably because it meant I had to free up head space and diary space to do so. I could not commit to it as achieving goal one meant bringing in more revenue.

We all knew we could not grow any further unless better systems enabled the team to support our work.

The third goal (that I did not achieve) was to end the year with 20% of my physical and mental energy reserves left in the tank. Ironically, if I had established the systems my team desperately tried to get me to do, I would have achieved this and significantly increased the achievement levels on goals one and two.

Some of us are slow to learn.

Systems are now a core focus of our team and business planning discussions. We use our software to its full capacity, creating business flows that enable the team to carry out relevant actions rather than relying on my brain to prompt them. That disentangles me from things I've clung to since starting my practice.

It was a hard reminder that systems are the stepping stones to reaching our goals and no matter how tempting it can feel, they cannot be ignored.

A simpler example relates to the goal of eating more nutritious food. An enabling system might be preparing multiple meals on

Sunday. This is an admirable goal, but unless you create a system to achieve it, it just stays in your head as a nice idea.

We've forgotten how to persist

We're so used to instant gratification that we give up unless the goal is achieved quickly.

The stonemason chips away at massive pieces of granite, day after day, with little visible progress. They continue, firm in the belief that sustained effort will bring results. And sure enough, one more little chip splits the granite in half. It wasn't that one blow that created the massive change; it was the continued effort of small blows.

How many of us tasked with splitting a chunk of granite would cast a few back-breaking blows, then throw down the tool and skulk away defeated when nothing seemed to change?

Authorship is a prime example of persistence, but while the overall goal is enormous, there are micro achievements and rewards along the way that help sustain our efforts. We use this same psychology in large-scale change to maintain momentum and motivation.

We don't celebrate the small steps

Some goals are long-term. Slow, microscopic, gradual shifts amount to enormous changes over time. Keep the momentum by finding ways to identify and celebrate those shifts, no matter how small.

Slow, microscopic, gradual shifts amount to enormous changes over time.

Use reflective practice such as journalling, keeping a gratitude diary, or answering questions (What are you most proud of? What worked well?) at the end of each day. These identify the micro shifts you may otherwise miss and sustain motivation for the longer journey.

Watch, too, for gradual shifts in your thinking. You might not recognise what's changed, just that you are thinking differently.

For example, in my Breakthrough workload management program, participants spend the first four weeks in the 'awareness' phase. Their task is to become aware of where their work is coming from and their habitual responses to requests.

When we reflect each week on their progress, we celebrate if someone recalls a time when they renegotiated priorities or proposed a task swap instead of saying yes to an additional task or project. This gradual shift in thinking is essential to sustainable workload management.

I'm a fan of these words from Calvin Coolidge, US President from 1923-29. 'Nothing in the world can take the place of persistence. Talent will not; nothing is more common than unsuccessful [people] with talent. Genius will not; unrewarded genius is almost a proverb. Education will not; the world is full of educated derelicts. Persistence and determination alone are omnipotent.'

We fail to take action

I use the KIA model in my workplace programs. Knowledge + Intention + Action = Change

Sitting through a workshop or training program does not create change. It provides knowledge to understand what change we want to make and how to go about doing so. But it does not actually make the change.

Action must be taken for change to occur. No amount of knowing how to run gets you from Point A to Point B. A running coach can build your technical knowledge, but you're still at Point A.

What's the intention?

Why do you want to run from A to B?

Why is it important?

Do you have an emotional investment in making that trip?

Will it benefit you in other ways?

Are you set on making this change?

What happens if you do?

What happens if you don't?

Unless you can emotionally invest in the outcome and set the intention to make the change, no amount of knowing how will matter. When you know how to do it, and set the intention, it's time to take action.

Break the inertia. Move off the starting block and propel yourself from point A to point B.

KIA. Knowledge + Intention + Action = Change

Your KIA plan

Throughout this book, there are loads of ideas you'll want to act on. Use the following table (Figure 7) to plot your ideas, set your intention and take action.

Wanting to change won't make it so.

Wanting to do it isn't enough. Wanting to change won't make it so. No amount of wishing will move you off the starting line.

List all the things you'd like to change or implement. Pick three. Break those down into 90-day action plans and focus on one step at a time.

Knowledge	Intention	Action
What have I learnt that I want to implement?	Why is this important to me? How will I feel when I do this? What will happen if I make this change? What if I don't? What's my level of emotional investment?	What's one action that will move me off the starting line? How will I build on that?

Knowledge	Intention	Action
E.g. I want to establish protected time.	*E.g. It will help my productivity and reduce my mental fatigue at the end of my work day. That means I can show up fresher for the family.*	*E.g. I'm going to tell my leader and my team that I'd like to pilot this, share why, and talk about the structure.*
E.g. I want to establish a regular cadence for 1:1 meetings	*E.g. I now know the benefits for me, my team and getting the work done.*	*E.g. I'm going to get the template from Tanya and meet with my team to set up the schedule, explaining why it's so important and will help us all.*

Figure 7: KIA action plan

Other hacks for action

Here are some things that have worked for me when I've wanted to set an intention and take action.

- ► visual reminders, goals, signage and photos
- ► Post-it notes on the bathroom mirror (these are surprisingly effective!)
- ► reminders in my phone or calendar
- ► identify any potential or likely barriers and make a plan to remove those before I start
- ► get an accountability buddy or coach.

'Give thanks to empty moments given to dreams, and for thoughtful people who help those dreams come true.'

– William Stanley Braithwaite

Part Three

Looking After Them

Now that you've identified how to keep yourself thriving sustainably, it's time to explore how to look after your team. That's a big part of how safe and effective leaders find equilibrium.

This section isn't about wrapping your people in cotton wool, providing indulgent environments or intalling coffee machines in every work space. It's about understanding the factors that engage and motivate your team, and keep them safe.

We are going deep on the topic of stress, to how this differs from stretch and strain. We will explore psychosocial hazards and why it's imperative to understand these, how they may interact and compound, and what to do about assessing and managing the risks.

Importantly, you will understand common misapplication of terminology and concepts that can leave leaders feeling disempowered and vulnerable when attempting to monitor or manage performance in accordance with reasonable management actions.

You'll learn why it is so important for you and your team to understand each other's strengths and the role those strengths play in mitigating work stress. You'll also understand how to manage social loafers and address other unhelpful behaviours that can impact your team culture.

Chapter Ten

The Changing Landscape

We know that work has a significant impact on mental wellbeing. However, evidence continues to show that workplaces are predominantly directing their wellbeing spend towards individual programs rather than tackling the systemic and structural elements known to create poor workplace mental health.

In February 2023, Dr Don McCreary released a white paper titled *Important Considerations for the Development of Workplace Mental Ill-health Prevention and Intervention Programs*. He wrote: 'Guidance documents from a wide range of diverse organisations ... all point to addressing workplace mental ill-health and burnout by focusing primarily on the structural, psychosocial barriers within organisations before implementing mental ill-health prevention or intervention programs for individual workers.'[40]

Psychosocial barriers

These barriers are called psychosocial hazards. These are aspects of work that may negatively impact people's psychological wellbeing. The presence of one of these hazards does not automatically signify an injury, but it indicates a higher risk of injury. Therefore, like physical hazards, there is a need to assess the identified risks and establish and review appropriate controls.

Australian organisations are responsible under national and state law and regulations. Codes of practice have been introduced in most jurisdictions to support workplaces to comply with their responsibilities. This has been significantly reinforced in recent years due to the escalating rates of mental injury as a result of unmanaged work-related stressors. I'll talk more about safety in Chapter 23.

What's within your control and influence

Leaders must build their knowledge of common psychosocial hazards and how these may be at play in the workplace and work teams.

> Employees now expect greater care and consideration for their psychological wellbeing.

Regulators insist upon it. Expectations have changed, and employees now expect greater care and consideration for their psychological wellbeing.

Over recent years, some employees have used this knowledge to their advantage and misapplied terms. That means leaders must confidently understand the topic so they can coach and support employees where necessary.

Chapter Eleven

Understanding Stretch, Stress and Strain

Safe Work Australia reports that workers experience stress when they perceive the demands of their work exceed their ability or resources to cope.[41]

Similarly, in *Atlas of the Heart,* Brené Brown writes that we feel stressed when we evaluate environmental demands as beyond our ability to cope successfully.[42] The WHO defines stress as a state of worry or mental tension caused by a difficult situation.[43] Most definitions talk about our evaluation of the stressful situation or demands around us (stress events) and our ability or resources to cope with these demands. We will explore resources in Chapter 24.

Not all stress is bad

However, there's a common workplace misconception that all stress is bad and no level of stress should be felt while carrying out our work duties and responsibilities. This is fundamentally incorrect. So it is essential that leaders clearly understand the types of stress, the factors that move stress into the high-risk zone and the differences between stretch, stress and strain.

Stretch

Increasingly, I support leaders who set stretch tasks for workers and are met with the response, 'This is stressing me out and impacting my mental health.' Sensitive to modern workplace expectations many leaders feel unsure of how to proceed when these moments arise.

Challenging or 'stretch' work tasks keep us stimulated and engaged and contribute to growth and development. It's like attending a yoga class – stretching should always be within an individual's capabilities.

> Stretching should always be within an individual's capabilities.

A safe and effective leader looks for opportunities for stretch tasks for team members, supporting and encouraging them.

Expanding our knowledge through stretch tasks can be uncomfortable and may create temporary positive stress (see below), but it should never create strain.

Know your team member and their baseline psychological wellbeing and any external factors at play. Check in, seek feedback, monitor and encourage your team member to help them successfully navigate the stretch task and learn and grow.

Stress

The response to stress events is both physical and psychological.

Physiologically, the body responds with an increased heart rate and increases in cortisol and adrenaline, two common stress hormones.[44] We essentially experience a threat response. The body's response to a threat creates heightened levels of energy and arousal that are part of everyday life and motivate and drive us to achieve goals.[45]

Everyday life is full of stress events. Generally speaking, when the stress event is over, our stress response resolves. Cortisol and adrenaline levels return to normal. This type of positive stress is referred to as eustress.

It's a positive form of stress that helps us learn, grow, strive and achieve what we want in life. Eustress motivates us to perform daily activities. As Dr Adam Fraser writes, we all need some stress to get out of bed every morning.[46] It is motivating rather than impactful because we tend to have control.

In a recent workshop, I asked if any participants had moved house. I suggested that while moving was stressful, it was generally short term and associated with autonomy and goal achievement, making it a positive stress event overall. Those participants who felt it was not positive agreed it depended upon whether they were forced to move or chose to.

Problems arise when stress is severe, prolonged or unmanaged.

To better understand this, imagine yourself at the gym. Lifting weight puts stress on your muscles, and then you put it down and remove the stress. But what would happen if you lifted a heavier weight and held it for longer without support or assistance?

Problems arise when stress is severe, prolonged or unmanaged.

Your body's coping ability may be compromised and result in muscle strain.

Psychological stress operates in the same way. The presence of stress itself is rarely the issue. However, severe, prolonged and unmanaged stress (toxic stress or distress) has the potential to result in adverse outcomes such as mental strain or injury.

Strain

Much like working out too hard at the gym, severe, prolonged or unmanaged work-related stress place us at high risk of psychological strain (injury). This may include anxiety, depression, post-traumatic stress disorder and sleep disorders.[47]

Misunderstanding work-related stress

The misapplication of concepts relating to work stress means leaders are apprehensive when responding to workers. And rightly so. Who could blame them? The stakes are high and without appropriate parameters and education, leaders are placed in increasingly vulnerable situations and expected to navigate with little or no direction or clarity.

Getting work outcomes requires leaders to understand the concept of work stress, and know how to identify and reduce the risks associated with work stressors.[48]

Not everyone responds the same way to stressful situations. After all, we are all complex and unique individuals. Our upbringing, personality traits, learned and ingrained coping mechanisms, knowledge and experiences, and our history and traumas all influence how we respond to stressful events.

So, too, our home and social circumstances, work environment, job demands, work relationships and leader's style, support and encouragement.

One size does not fit all. That's why we see significant variability in response to the same event in the workplace and shake our heads in wonder. We're incredulous and desperately wish for consistency across the team so we can regulate our approach.

One size does not fit all.

The common approach is to blame individuals when a negative stress response presents itself. But more than one thing can be true here. You may have an individual who is not coping or regulating well and has other factors going on outside of work. Work may also be responsible for unreasonable levels of work-related stress that you can control.

Part of your role is to monitor the psychological wellbeing of your team. Below are some suggestions for doing this effectively.

Leaders support good stress and reduce bad stress

Safe and effective leaders know that dealing with stress is part of their responsibilities. So, what actions should you take to monitor and measure stress?

Ask: Regularly check in with your team members and ask how they are doing.

Use a scale: A wellbeing rating scale can assess their level of coping, feelings of stress or overwhelm. If you don't have one, the Super Six questions in Chapter 17 may be useful.

Don't judge: The key is to monitor regularly, privately and systematically. Ask questions without judgement or bias and support a positive resolution if someone says they're struggling. Gallup's 2023 State of the Australian and New Zealand Workplace report indicated that five out of ten Australian workers were experiencing 'a lot' of stress, and 67% of Australian workers said they were quiet quitting – meaning they were showing up but doing the bare minimum.[49]

Annual surveys: Most organisations use some form of annual survey tool to assess worker engagement, satisfaction and stress. Questions within these surveys often elicit meaningful data for organisations. Leaders cannot always access the full reports or dashboards and may only receive consolidated data. They rarely have discrete team data due to survey construction that protects anonymity. I encourage you to do further reviews with your team. Check the completion rates of any surveys you may review and be wary of explaining poor results away.

Chapter Twelve

Your Positive Influence

Broadly speaking, mental wellbeing is influenced by personality traits, strengths, proactivity and history. Alongside home and social factors, the workplace can play a disproportionate part, given how much time people spend at work, in work, or ruminating over work. Who hasn't spent a restless night reliving a frustrating interaction?

Given this, what can leaders do? While there's a lot you can't control, there are many areas you can positively influence.

Organisational psychologist Arnold Bakker, from the University of Rotterdam, examined the role of positive leadership as a potential remedy for job burnout. He found that healthy leadership may help employees regulate short-term fatigue and avoid enduring burnout.[50] Given work plays such a large role in most of our lives, it stands to reason that leadership can have a positive impact – even without formal evidence from experts such as Professor Bakker.

What can you influence?

You may have an opportunity to influence the subculture of your team or those you have inter-dependencies with. How you interact with each other and the behaviours you model all create a positive influence. However, your influence on your direct reports is even more impactful as work intersects with their individual traits and personalities, as well as their home and social lives.

How can you influence individual factors?

In Chapter 15, I write extensively about the benefits of helping individuals **understand their unique strengths** and the team and organisational insights you can also obtain. When we play to our strengths, we are more likely to find ourselves in flow in our work and be energised, engaged and motivated. If our roles require us to use lesser strengths, this can impact our energy, commitment to the job or task, or overall organisation.

This is beyond finding the right person for the role. It's understanding people's unique talents and identifying opportunities (special tasks, projects, activities) that best use their strengths. While we're on the subject, remember that people bring other skills to the table that can enrich their working lives. For example, an artist could lead their team in a 'paint and sip' afternoon or create new artwork for the office walls.

> Coaching brings out the best in people.

Coaching brings out the best in people, not telling or commanding. We'll dig more into this in Chapter 16.

Communicate regularly, transparently and effectively with your team members so they know what's happening and what to expect. What's your vehicle for communicating? Do you send regular communiqués? Do you check in with your team each morning, for example, via a toolbox talk or a huddle?

How do you ensure transparent and frequent communication with your team? Is that system the right fit for them? Being open to suggestions from team members is also a powerful influence on wellbeing.

Informal **job crafting** identifies ways they may wish to tweak their roles. Their ideas can provide great insights into pain points that can be reduced or removed with small changes. By listening and encouraging team members to offer suggestions, you are giving them agency over the demands of their role. This autonomy is pivotal in reducing work stress.

How can you influence their home and social environment?

When we experience severe stress at work, we rarely take our best selves through the door when we get home. Our loved ones are very good at identifying when things are getting to us at work. Sometimes, they notice before we do. When we head home mentally drained, with nothing left in the tank and a short fuse, there's bound to be a ripple effect.

Leaders have more influence in this space than they think. Your awareness of how each team member is tracking can reduce their work/home conflict:

What can you do?

Set reasonable expectations around working hours and shifts done outside normal working hours. Offer flexibility for child-raising responsibilities, caring or other factors that are important to the individual. Of course, such flexibility needs to be within organisational policies and procedures, and balanced with reliability and accountability. Watch for any impact on operational requirements and other team members. This can be complex to navigate.

Give appropriate feedback to reduce uncertainty around job performance or job sustainability. Addressing underperformance means no one carries an unreasonable burden.

Regularly check workload volumes, priorities and timelines. Negotiate these as necessary to reduce severe stress.

Think about what you *can* do – rather than what you can't. While much is outside your control, there's still a great deal of positive impact you can make as a safe and effective leader.

Chapter Thirteen

Beware Fundamental Attribution Errors

When witnessing poor behaviours at work, it's easy to blame individual personality or disposition. It's what social psychologists call 'fundamental attribution error'. It's a bias that occurs when we decide that an individual's personality attributes are responsible rather than situational factors that include the environment, other people involved, the moment or event and the context.

We need to take a broader view of individual behavioural responses and look at workplace culture, psychosocial hazards and current events that provide additional context.

The following case study offers a deeper understanding.

Share the load

Peter was a busy leader who had just landed an additional organisation-wide project. He wanted to enlist Lapinda, one of his top performers, to support the design and implementation. Peter was confident that she would be a superstar to help achieve this project.

The team had been particularly busy of late, but Peter knew that Lapinda loved to be challenged. She was highly qualified and experienced and never missed deadlines or delivered shoddy work. A perfectionist, Lapinda never said no and always went above and beyond. When Peter asked her to mentor two other team members to lift the quality of their work, it ruffled some feathers in the team. Lapinda had a bit of a rough time with them, but he was sure that they would get over it.

Peter arranged to meet with Lapinda and brief her on the additional project. At first, Lapinda listened attentively, but as the conversation continued, she appeared visibly angry. Her posture was rigid and her face stern.

Peter was surprised when Lapinda asked, 'Well, what am I going to drop to focus on this project?' Normally, she would just add it to her load and work until it was done. He smiled and said, 'You know how it is, no money, so we just have to get it done. It's come from the top.'

Lapinda snapped, 'I can't do it all. You need to stop loading me up all the time.' She got up abruptly, saying, 'Get one of the other team to do it. We all get paid the same – why don't they get the same workload?' and walked out.

Peter was completely shocked by Lapinda's response. 'That was unregulated behaviour and I expected more from her,' he muttered.

As he mulled over the incident, he began to think a little less of Lapinda and wondered if he'd exaggerated her achievements in the past. She was clearly not the high performer he believed she was.

Let's analyse this event.

Remember that a fundamental attribution error occurs when we decide that the individual's personality or attributes are responsible for the behaviour – rather than the situational context.

In the Peter and Lapinda scenario, we know these facts:

► Lapinda is a top performer, predisposed to taking on additional tasks for Peter and working extra hours to complete extra demands.

► Lapinda has some tension with her team, having been asked to mentor them on the quality of their work.

► She has worked hard for a long time; this was not a one-off request.

► Given Lapinda's history of meeting his extra demands, Peter's expectations are high.

► Lapinda has not previously responded in this manner when asked to take on extra demands.

► Lapinda's behaviour outside of this event has been perfectly fine.

What conclusions can you draw from this scenario? Is Lapinda's personality the cause of this encounter with Peter, or could something else be the cause? Consider the following factors:

Lapinda is currently having an awkward time with her team after Peter's request that she mentor them to improve their quality of work. Could this be creating some extra pressure and worry for her? Could this impact her relationships with her colleagues?

Peter has singled Lapinda out yet again for a special project. Given what's happening within the team, might she be concerned that she is seen as the favourite?

Lapinda has been working very hard for a long time, always saying yes and delivering top performance. Is there a limit to her capacity?

Is it fair that Lapinda should continue to take on extra tasks without additional support or ability to negotiate her priorities?

Assessing causation

There are three factors to consider when determining whether we can attribute someone's behaviour to internal or external causes.

Consistency: Does this person usually behave this way in this situation?

Distinctiveness: Does this person behave differently in this situation than in others?

Consensus: Do others behave similarly in this situation?

If you apply these three considerations, what is your conclusion? Can we attribute Lapinda's behaviour to her personality/disposition or her situation?

The answer is *the situation*.

A broader view

We must always consider the work-related stress risks of psychosocial hazards and how stress can negatively impact individual behaviours. Don't fall victim to fundamental attribution errors when responding to events in the workplace. Take a broader view of the situation.

Chapter Fourteen

Eradicate Common Culture Killers

'Everyone is a cultural architect of the workplace.'
– Timothy R. Clark[51]

It can be convenient to point the finger up, down or horizontally in your workplace when cultural concerns exist. The reality, however, is that everyone contributes to culture through attitudes, moods and behaviours.

> Everyone contributes to culture through attitudes, moods and behaviours.

Leading safely and effectively requires you to know this and to ensure positive modelling, as well as setting and holding the line on behavioural expectations. Essentially, you eradicate the common culture killers within teams and, more broadly, in the workplace.

Here are three common culture killers you should be on top of.

Disrespectful, disparaging and discriminatory behaviours

Your role is to use respectful and inclusive language and call out disrespectful, disparaging or discriminatory behaviours. This is particularly important as issues such as work-related gendered violence surface, along with data that continues to show patterns of discrimination – particularly against Aboriginal and Torres Strait Islanders and those identifying as LGBTQIA+.[52]

> Helping various generations appreciate and value what each brings to the team will be vital in ensuring a harmonious team culture.

Navigating workforce age diversity is an additional challenge. As people stay at work longer, generational differences are revealed in working styles, values, beliefs and attitudes. Helping various generations appreciate and value what each brings to the team will be vital in ensuring a harmonious team culture.

Draw on the strengths of those who are skilled and speedy in graphic design and technology. Discuss concepts such as crystallised intelligence, which refers to knowledge, facts and skills accumulated throughout life.[53] This rich knowledge is a gift if harnessed and channelled in the right way. Encourage people of all ages in your team to respect each other's strengths.

Incivility

Incivility describes pervasive, divisive behaviours that seep into the fabric of teams and workplaces, creating deep-seated resentments and toxic behaviours. It is the lack of courtesy. It is rudeness, an impolite act or remark. Incivility kills helpfulness and collaboration.[54]

While incivility is not always intentional, it signals a lack of care for the person you are communicating with, whether written, verbal or non-verbal.

Passive-aggressive behaviours such as eye-rolling, head-shaking and looking bored when someone is speaking can create conflict. Other common points of tension within teams can be emails sent without salutations or with a blunt message. Being directive (perceived or real) as a peer can also cause problems.

> **Incivility kills helpfulness and collaboration.**

Acts of incivility include not greeting people, excluding, gossiping and undermining others, not showing appreciation and general rudeness.

Canadian researchers have identified significant issues associated with incivility. When unchecked, incivility is often met with more of the same, impacting people's enjoyment and motivation to participate and, therefore, team cohesion and effectiveness.

Figure 8 shows a great visual for your team to boost civility. You can download this graphic for free from the resources section of my website. https://tanyaheaneyvoogt.com/resources/

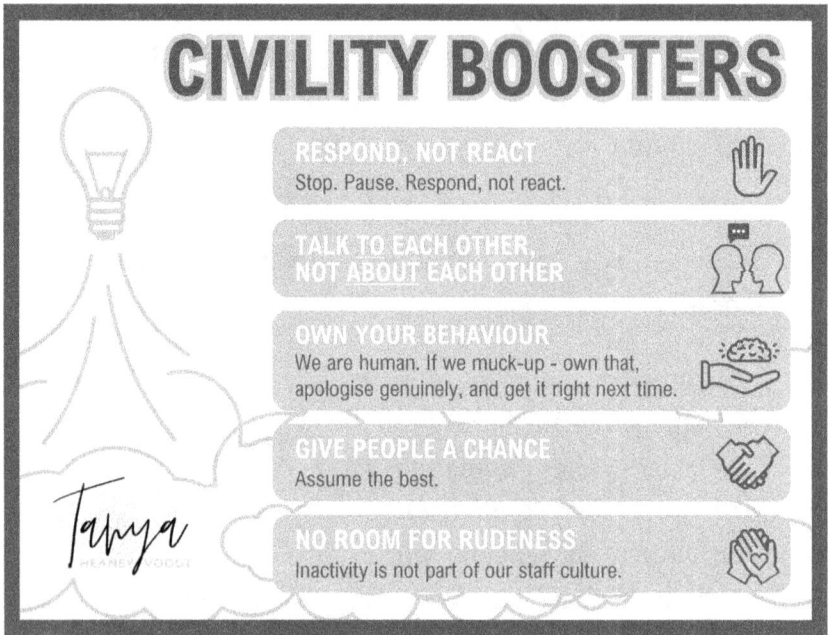

CIVILITY BOOSTERS

RESPOND, NOT REACT
Stop. Pause. Respond, not react.

TALK TO EACH OTHER, NOT ABOUT EACH OTHER

OWN YOUR BEHAVIOUR
We are human. If we muck-up - own that, apologise genuinely, and get it right next time.

GIVE PEOPLE A CHANCE
Assume the best.

NO ROOM FOR RUDENESS
Inactivity is not part of our staff culture.

Figure 8: Civility boosters

Social loafing

Do you feel that someone in your workgroup isn't pulling their weight?

Social psychologists refer to this behaviour as social loafing and define it as 'the tendency for individuals to exert less effort when they pool their efforts (towards a common goal) than when they are individually accountable.[55]

Researchers have explored social loafing for more than a century and have identified that this behaviour occurs more readily when an individual feels, or is perceived as 'lost in the crowd'. One of the most notable studies was conducted in 1913 and involved a rope tug-of-war experiment. When groups were assigned to each side, group effort was half the sum of individual efforts.

Other studies have confirmed that we are inclined to reduce individual efforts when our endeavours are pooled.

> We are inclined to reduce individual efforts when our endeavours are pooled.

Common workplace scenarios where social loafing may occur include functional or cross-functional work teams, committees, project or working groups and other group-based activities.

There are implications within work groups too, when a colleague is perceived as not contributing equally, leading to resentment and conflict, and impacting team and cross-team culture.

If you've always said you work better alone, you're probably vigorously strumming your air guitar right now. But group work is an essential part of our working life, and we need to be aware of and address the conditions that may precipitate social loafing to realise the brilliance of collective intelligence.

When the conditions are ripe

There are three conditions when social loafing is likely to occur:

First, when people feel their efforts don't matter or will go unnoticed. 'If my efforts can't be measured or observed, how do

I and others know I am contributing to the outcome?' This can demotivate some individuals from bringing their best.

Second, research has shown that social loafing increases if participants deem a task is too easy.

The third situation is when free riders jump on board. These people don't feel they need to put in as much (or any) effort in the group as others will carry the load, so they sit back and enjoy the ride. The belief leading to this behaviour can be conscious or unconscious and trigger others to disengage, leading to poorer overall group performance.

Minimising social loafing

Eliminating social loafing is a bigger task than you might think. However, there are ways to discourage and minimise it.

Make individual performance identifiable

Think about who gets the acknowledgement when committees, discrete teams and project groups achieve outcomes. Are individuals recognised for their role? Or are they collectively acknowledged as members of the group?

Acknowledgement is about feedback on the task – not generally about public accolades. We get a sense of achievement from seeing the part we play.

Can people choose tasks that interest them? Sometimes, we are voluntold to attend, compromising engagement and motivation from the get-go. Try listing the tasks required and asking people to choose what they want to work on. Communicate the list of mini-tasks or projects so people know their contributions can be identified.

Clarify roles and responsibilities within the group. Making individual performance identifiable also means you can identify those who are not contributing so appropriate action can be taken.

Make group tasks challenging, appealing and involving

Hard tasks increase stress levels and create arousal, which lifts performance and assists us in meeting the challenge. This happens every day without us being aware.

If you're bored at work, that means the work you're doing isn't challenging you. You're under-stimulated. The same happens with group tasks that are too easy. The brain sends a whispering message that says it's not motivating enough to exert any effort. No one will notice as others will do the work. So, in athletic terms, we don't get off the starting blocks.

> If you're bored at work, that means the work you're doing isn't challenging you.

Motivation theories tell us that it is the outcome that matters to individuals. Effort, and therefore performance, is directly attributable to the perceived outcome. Social loafing is more likely to occur if the group activity and anticipated outcome hold no individual appeal.

Have you ever exerted less effort in a group because you felt like an outsider? Most of us have; it's a natural human response. Being actively included can reduce the chances of social loafing and provide a raft of other benefits associated with inclusive teams. We all need to feel a sense of inclusion and belonging.

Social loafing is a negative group phenomenon and should be avoided wherever possible. While individual traits may also influence behaviours and motivation, be aware of the conditions in which social loafing is more likely to occur. Implementing known strategies should ensure that collective performance far outweighs individual.

Chapter Fifteen

Know Your Strengths

It is a cliché to 'Know your strengths'. We see it emblazoned across LinkedIn platforms, job advertisements, newsletters and other media. Leaders use it. Sports coaches scream, 'Play to your strengths', and we all smile and nod as though we know what they are talking about.

Most of us have some general awareness or belief about our strengths. But it's not usually specific. We might say, 'Yes, I'm good at working with people' or 'I'm good with spreadsheets', but is that enough?

What about you? Can you list your top five strengths? Other people are usually far more aware of our strengths than we are. We can understand areas for improvement or development if we are open to hearing constructive feedback delivered with positive intent.

What about an area you don't know about – a blind spot? These areas you may be unaware of are also generally obvious to others. These behaviours, traits and habits may get in the way of your success. As with strengths, feedback, delivered well by trusted parties, can reveal your blindspots.

Johari Window

This concept of things known and unknown to you and others is well depicted in the Johari Window Model (Figure 9), developed in 1955 by American psychologists Joseph Luft and Harry Ingham.

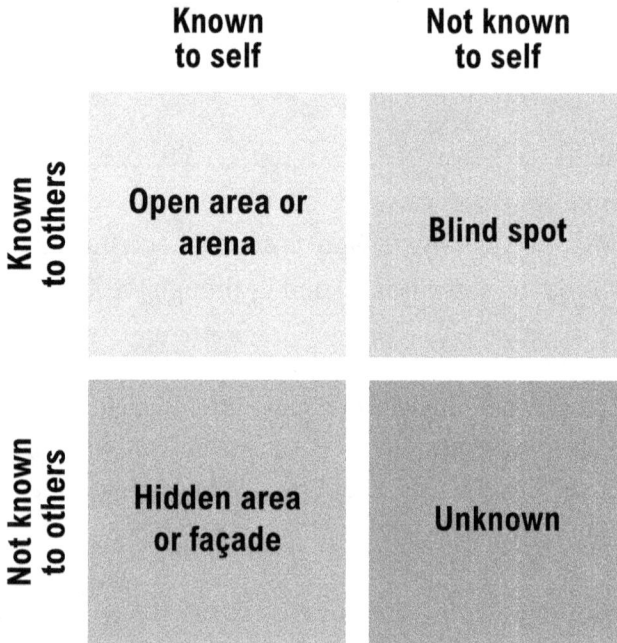

	Known to self	Not known to self
Known to others	Open area or arena	Blind spot
Not known to others	Hidden area or façade	Unknown

Figure 9: Johari Window model

The model was traditionally used to enhance team communication, citing the importance of seeking and providing feedback to reduce blind spots and unknown areas. While it's somewhat dated, I still find it useful to demonstrate how we can be unaware of our traits and choose not to reveal parts of ourselves.

Let me explain.

The top left quadrant is the open area or arena. It contains information about your attitudes, behaviours, emotions, feelings, skills and views that are known by you *and* those around you.

The top right quadrant is your blind spot. These are the things that others may know about you – but you are blind to. For example, they may know you are exceedingly task-focused, which can sometimes impact relationships. Or, conversely, you display so much empathy for your team members that you may be hesitant to manage performance appropriately.

The lower left quadrant includes what is hidden. This is information that you know but you keep from others. It might be personal information and include feelings, past experiences, fears and worries. Perhaps you feel that you never have enough information or time to appropriately research a matter before making a decision. Or that your tendency to overthink or over-analyse can make you work slower.

The unknown area is in the bottom right quadrant. It is information that no one is aware of. This could be feelings, talents or strengths you have yet to discover, and that others have not observed in you.

Be careful what you focus on

Any informal approach to strengths identification is useful. However, a better way to understand how you and others tick is to understand your natural strengths through a scientifically validated assessment instrument. One that facilitates

No one likes to hear they aren't good at something.

constructive conversations amongst team members and reduces tensions and conflicts that arise when feedback is delivered poorly.

There are many weakness-focused instruments designed to enhance self-awareness. While they may achieve this, they can have a significant negative impact. No one likes to hear they aren't good at something. Covert tools such as the 360 can often yield cruel feedback that pulls the rug out from underneath well-meaning leaders.

One executive came to me for coaching when she was devastated by a scathing 360 assessment that completely blindsided her and left her doubting her abilities to the point of paralysis.

Look for what's right

'What would happen if we studied what was right with people, versus what's wrong with people?'

That powerful question was asked by Don Clifton, the American psychologist, educator and researcher. Clifton started his research at the University of Nebraska-Lincoln library. But he was struck that all the psychology books were about what is wrong with people. He couldn't find a single one about what might be right.[56]

From 1949 until he died in 2003, Clifton researched and invented ways to help people maximise their potential. He was determined to help people understand who they are and who they could become. His work ultimately led to the development of the Clifton Strengths Assessment (formerly known as Clifton StrengthsFinder). This evidence-based assessment tool is underpinned by 60 years of research.

Over 31 million people worldwide have completed the assessment, including more than 90% of Fortune 500 companies. I have used this assessment in my work for years. It never fails to impress me and those who utilise it. The tool provides rich understanding of why interpersonal relationships may be tense or unproductive.

Let's see how.

Marco and Kerry had been at odds with each other for months. As Kerry's new director, Marco's style rubbed her up the wrong way. Marco did all he could to engage her and couldn't understand why Kerry was so obstructive.

Frustration and tension were high.

I was Marco's executive coach. We had undertaken his Clifton Strengths Assessment, so I suggested it may be a good idea for Kerry to do it too. She was willing and the results made it clear why tensions had arisen.

Marco is high in executing talents – he is task/output focused. Kerry is high in relationship building talents – she gets the job done through building relationships. After being in her role for decades, Kerry was naturally protective of her team and Marco's task-based, take-action approach set off flares.

Fortunately, they both had a sincere desire to improve their working relationship. With their permission, I held 1:1 meetings with them and unpacked their results in the context of the relationship tensions they were experiencing.

Kerry agreed that, at times, she found it hard to manage the performance of team members and could over-empathise with them. She gets the work done, but the people are generally her first consideration and she can get buried in the emotions. Kerry said she would find it useful to have support from Marco and coaching when she had to make tough decisions.

An impressively open and self-aware leader, Marco clearly saw where he could benefit from Kerry's strengths. She taught him a more relational aspect, which was valuable when trying to influence changes in his directorate and the organisation. The assessment and discussions showed that Kerry and Marco were valued in the team and their unique strengths are important. Each brings something essential to the table; there is no 'my way or the highway' approach.

Understanding their Strengths profiles showed they could be a formidable team if they pooled their unique talents.

After our individual meetings, Marco and Kerry got together to share their results. They decompressed with a laugh as they realised why they had gotten off on the wrong foot. Respect soared as they saw the value in each other's profiles and how they could draw on each other to be more successful in their roles.

Kerry and Marco went on to work extremely well together. It is an absolute credit to them that they were open and honest enough with each other and themselves to achieve this outcome. One of the keys to this success was addressing the situation early before deep resentments could form.

I have long used the Gallup Clifton Strengths 34 profile tool with individuals and teams, and it continues to impress with meaningful insights. Team maps can provide useful organisational data and assist in designing programs and interventions that bring out the best in the workforce.

Organisational insights

We can gain valuable organisational insights into strengths when working with teams and across organisations.

At one organisation, I mapped the individual and collective strengths profiles of the CEO and executive team. The report showed that more than 75% of the group had a strength that required more 1:1 time and deeper connections. These individuals were geographically spread and remote from one another, and relationships were not as strong as they could have been. Through this and other identifying patterns, they understood their current state culture and designed activities to achieve their desired future state.

In another organisation, we profiled almost 80% of their leadership and identified that the natural strengths of the group signalled a higher risk of overwork and burnout. This group needed support to ensure they took appropriate breaks, and the executive team needed to monitor the levels of discretionary effort they contributed because of their innate strengths.

On a personal level, understanding my Strengths profile helped me understand why I love developing people but need to lock myself away and stay in my head for hours on end. That insight was totally revealing and gave me permission to do what is necessary to play to my strengths. It stopped me from feeling anti-social because I needed those moments of alone time.

'I always felt there was something wrong with me' were the relieved words one executive used after completing the instrument. Understanding the gifts of our strengths, means we recognise that they make us who we are. These are science-backed answers, not some personality flaw.

I've seen incredible transformations using this instrument for individuals, functional teams and broader leadership teams.

We all tick differently.

We all tick differently. We are all unique and beautiful and complex and sometimes annoying. Understanding yourself better allows you to work in ways that energise you and develop patterns and habits that bring out your best. Doing that helps your team do the same.

Introverts and extroverts

One personality trait that some instruments measure is introversion and extroversion. Most of us know whether we get energy from or away from people. Yet, recently, we've seen a meshing of these traits, which I think better represents reality.

For example, I'm an extrovert who regularly likes to hide away from the world to recharge my batteries. Does that make me an introverted extrovert or an extroverted introvert? Or just someone who knows how to regulate their energy? You can see the problem.

These categories can create some confusion in other ways, too. It's generally well-accepted that introverts need quiet, thinking time. They absolutely do. But they're not the only ones.

Thinking time is for all

We regularly encounter people with deep thinking and processing talents in our strengths-based work. Such talents mean these individuals need time to think – and many identify as extroverts.

People high in strategic thinking talents are often introspective, deep inside their minds, following a thread or ruminating on an issue. They may appear quiet in team meetings or training workshops and be mistaken as disinterested or disengaged, but they are fully present, listening to the wheels turning in their brains. They're taking everything in, processing in their way.

People with these talents need time to process to produce their best ideas. Yet, in a synchronous world, we often give them mere moments to do so.

In my psychological safety workshops, we do a breakout activity where small teams list things they've seen that shut down people's ability to contribute ideas, solutions and suggestions in teams or workplaces. Without fail, the issue of 'thinking time' is raised every time. Generally, in the guise of 'time for different styles to process' or 'time outside the meeting to provide feedback'.

One simple way to enable everyone to bring their best ideas to the table is to give them a precursor – some

Those who process deeply are worth hearing from.

preliminary information. That means sharing the problem before coming together to create solutions. Give people time to prepare and ruminate and process, so when they show up to your meeting, they're bringing formed ideas.

Of course, the onus is on them to do that preparation.

If your meetings are quiet, perhaps this is the missing element. Yes, it will mean you must change how you do things, but that's necessary if you want diverse contributions. And surely those who process deeply are worth hearing from.

Chapter Sixteen

Coach for Growth and Accountability

The International Coaching Federation (ICF) defines coaching as partnering with clients in a thought-provoking and creative process that inspires them to maximise their personal and professional potential.[57]

Coaching is a way of bringing out the best in people. It deepens thinking, challenges limiting beliefs and shows there are other ways to look at life. It is not the outdated form of performance management it was once considered, so you may need to clarify the concept if you are talking about coaching for your team members. It is still shaking off negative connotations.

> Coaching is a key contemporary skill required of leaders.

From a leadership perspective, it is recognised that coaching is a key contemporary skill required of leaders. We coach, not tell. We help people come to their own conclusions.

According to Timothy R. Clark, social scientist, researcher and author, not everyone may be coachable.[58] Clark states that an individual needs emotional intelligence and a desire to change. But there are different levels of coaching and the questions we use range from deep and thought-provoking to the everyday responses leaders can use to reframe negative thinking and challenge habitual patterns.

The golden rules of coaching

There are three key principles to follow when you are coaching.

Don't ask 'Why...?' Instead, use 'How', 'Where', 'Tell me', 'Do you'.

Stay out of the space: This can be tricky at first. When we ask a coaching question, we pause. We get comfortable with silence. We hold our hands and our tongues and don't fill the space. This moment of silence is gold. It is very hard for problem-solvers and people-pleasers who want others to feel comfortable. We want to end the silence, so we jump in and give answers. But that ruins the process and the effectiveness of the coaching question.

> Stay out of the space.

Practice makes this easier. Your body language will also help, so make sure your posture is relaxed and open.

Listen actively: When we listen actively, we aren't solving the problem or formulating a response; we are simply listening. This takes a lot of practice and is one of the hardest aspects of coaching. For now, just be aware of it. That's a start.

General coaching questions

These are useful questions to learn about your people.

► What challenges do you anticipate, and how can we prepare for them? (Sets the expectation that challenges are normal and that we can prepare and overcome them.)

► How do you prefer to receive feedback, and how can I best support you in reaching your potential? (Normalises the role of feedback and shows an openness to help develop others.)

> What would feeling appreciated look like for you?

► What motivates you, and how can we align your personal goals with team and organisational objectives? (Helps people to tap into their 'why' and shows your intention to support them to achieve their personal and work-related goals.)

► How can we work together to ensure that everyone on the team feels valued and included? (Sets the basis for inclusion and demonstrates your expectations of how you want the team to feel.)

► Do you feel that your work is appreciated? What would feeling appreciated look like for you? (Opens up a powerful conversation to provide positive feedback in a way that ensures individuals feel valued and important.)

► What motivates you to come to work each day? (Helps you understand individual needs and motivations so you can tap into these if you feel motivation wavers.)

- What is your favourite part of your job? (Some roles have a lot of demands. Keep people focused on the elements of their role that they love, to sustain motivation and a positive mindset.)

- Which aspects of your job drain you? Which aspects energise you? Is there a balance? (Sets the expectation that there will always be drainers, but to maximise engagement and motivation, you'll want to see that balanced with energisers. Explore what drainers you can remove.)

Specific questions to build accountability and responsibility

These questions solve the 'dump and run' problem.

- What specifically, are you trying to achieve?

- What have you tried so far?

- What other options are there? *(If the answer is 'I don't know', respond with 'That's okay, take your time to think about it. Who might know? Where might you get answers? How could you find out?')*

- What will you try? How will you move forward?

Reframing

Reframing is a fabulous concept that supports mental wellbeing. The basic idea is to turn a negative into a positive.

It's not about false or toxic positivity; it's about seeing both sides of the coin. We are naturally wired to see the negative (the threat), so we need to balance things out and remember that there can always be a positive.

> ## It's easy to get stuck in a fixed negative mindset.

It's easy to get stuck in a fixed negative mindset, repeating what we've always said or heard and thinking that we believe it. But that's not always the case. Coaching helps lift the lid on that. Here are some common workplace-based examples with responses that reframe them.

I don't have time.

- ► Where could you find the time?
- ► How could you carve out the time? What could you let go of?
- ► Who else has time?
- ► When might you have the time?
- ► Where is your time going at the moment?
- ► What are you currently working on that you feel isn't your top priority?

We've always done it that way.

- ► What would happen if we tried it another way?
- ► Where can we do it differently?
- ► Where can we improve?
- ► Who has done it that way?

- ▶ What's the reason behind doing it that way?

- ▶ How long ago was that?

- ▶ How long have we been doing it this way for?

- ▶ How would it look if we changed it?

- ▶ Always? (This is a distortion – an emotive generalisation – see more about that below).

I don't know.

- ▶ That's okay, take your time.

- ▶ Tell me what you do know about this topic?

(This is the first line of defence; it's reactive, not thinking.)

This is too hard.

- ▶ How could we make it easier?

- ▶ What would make it easier?

(Easier is not the same as easy. We don't want people to give up at the first sign of a challenge. It's not about easy, but it's about achievable.)

Coaching through change

Try these key coaching questions to reframe negative comments in response to a change initiative:

- ▶ What do you think is driving the need for this change? Or: What do you think is the organisation's reason for this change?

- What, specifically, makes you uncomfortable about this change?
- Can you think of a time when you were hesitant about a change that turned out well?
- What learning from last time could help us be more successful this time?
- What would happen if we don't change?
- How could we make it easier for you?

> # What learning from last time could help us be more successful this time?

- What are the opportunities for you in this change?
- What will happen if you do make this change?

Challenging distortions

Distortions are sweeping emotive statements such as *'They don't care about us'*, *'Nobody knows what's going on'*, *'Everyone thinks it's stupid'* or *'It won't make any difference'*.

Try these coaching questions in response.

Distortion	Sample response
They don't care about us!	Who, specifically, doesn't care about whom?
Nobody knows what's going on!	Who does know?

Distortion	Sample response
Everyone thinks it's stupid.	Who, specifically, is everyone? What, specifically about this change do they think is stupid?
It won't make any difference. It won't work!	What would happen if it did? What suggestions do you have that will make a difference?
We tried this before and it didn't work!	What did you learn then that could help us be more successful this time? What has changed since then? What can you do, or what role can you play to ensure we are more successful this time? In other words, is everything else still the same? Time moves on and everything evolves around us. If we don't change, we become stagnant.

Chapter Seventeen

Communication and The Super Six

Make it regular and consistent

Regularly and systematically checking in with your team members is essential.

Irrespective of location (satellite site, home, across the globe), a regular communication structure is essential to provide the support, clarity and direction necessary for team members. This applies whether they are task workers, knowledge workers or subject matter experts.

At a minimum, conduct structured 1:1s every month, using a standard template or tool consistently across all team members. This will allow you to monitor progress, track actions (yours and your team member's) and record issues raised during these meetings. Make sure to retain these records as they are confirmation of agreed actions.

Have regular, quick check-ins via phone, email, in-person, text, or whatever tools are available to you. While these touch points are informal, they need to be intentional and not just 'if you have time'.

Distributed and 24/7 roster teams

In a recent coaching session, a leadership coaching client told me they personally phoned each team member about roster change requests rather than using the usual messaging app.

Staff working 24/7 shifts is common in health, hospitality and other industries. That means the leader is not always (or rarely) present for night or weekend shift staff and does not have the same depth of relationship with many of the staff.

The leader explained that phoning each staff member is an opportunity to connect and understand what is going on in their lives – how their family is, what events they are participating in, and how they are travelling.

While the calls achieve a work outcome, i.e., clarity on roster availability, these conversations deepen personal relationships, showing care and compassion for team members. They feel valued because the boss phoned rather than sent an impersonal text message.

In the modern world of work, teams are distributed across the globe and even more are working in hybrid or fully virtual ways. And technology has advanced to keep up with that. If you are based in Canada and have a team member in Australia, you must navigate a tricky time difference if you want to connect via phone. But you can still make this happen once a month.

Record and send video messages via a YouTube link or WhatsApp in the intervening weeks. The video message app Marco Polo provides a great visual connection that feels like real-time and is more interactive than pushing out a one-way video message.

Technology is surpassing workplace readiness, so lean in and take advantage of that to create efficiencies and effectiveness in communicating with your teams.

Make it more than casual

'Yes, I do have regular 1:1s with my team. I see them every day.'

This is a common response when leaders tell me about their schedule of check-ins with team members.

If your team are co-located and you do see them face-to-face every day, these are wonderful opportunities to keep your finger informally on the pulse. But these water-cooler, or corridor, moments aren't replacements for more meaningful conversations.

When leaders are in close contact with their team members, they often dispense with more structured individual meetings because they worry it is overkill. That's a valid concern. Death by meeting is a common risk for many workers.

> Formalised, structured 1:1s using a standard template are *essential.*

Informal, regular check-ins of any form are an essential part of your support routine. But formalised, structured monthly (or fortnightly in some instances) 1:1s using a standard template are *essential.*

One does not negate the other. Both are necessary.

Drop the excuses

'But I don't have time.' Make time. It's as simple as that.

Well, actually, there's more.

Let's consider the return on investment of that time. Proactively holding these conversations offers many benefits to you and your team members.

> This will reduce interruptions throughout your day as people will hold off their little queries until you meet.

They enable you to remediate little issues before they turn into big sticky ones – including wellbeing concerns.

They provide opportunities to clarify work priorities and understand barriers that may be getting in the way of team success. This will reduce interruptions throughout your day as people will hold off their little queries until you meet. Try it – I guarantee this will happen.

From a relational perspective, these conversations establish open and trusted communication and maintain a positive working relationship with your team members, enhancing your working life and theirs.

These conversations provide rich coaching opportunities to empower your team and reframe negative or unhelpful thinking. There's more about coaching in the next section.

Plan and prepare for your conversations ahead of time, particularly where corrective feedback may be required, to ensure you achieve the desired outcomes.

If you still need convincing, let's talk leadership support.

As you will read in Part Four: Getting The Work Done, leadership support is instrumental in generating high levels of performance, engagement, motivation and safety.

There are many elements in leadership support. Regular check-ins and formal 1:1s are the vehicles for looking after your team members and getting the work done.

The Super Six

These are the six best questions (with additional prompts) to ask regularly in your 1:1s.

1. What has been your greatest accomplishment this month?

2. What is your biggest challenge right now? What steps have you taken so far to address this challenge? What other options can you explore? How can I support you to overcome this challenge?

3. Quality improvement opportunities: What could we do differently to be more effective as a team?

4. Do you require any resources or equipment to achieve your goals? How could this be funded?

5. How can I help you be successful in your role? Discuss skills development, support needs, ways of

working together, items needing escalation and workload management.

6. How are you (and your team) travelling right now? Struggling? Doing okay but challenged? Good? Thriving? Are there any work-related stress factors we need to discuss? Any wellbeing concerns? What can we do to improve the rating (if struggling or challenged)? Are you clear on the support available for you and your team? What challenges do we need to unpack and address? How can I support you and your team?

> How are you (and your team) travelling right now? Struggling? Doing okay but challenged? Good? Thriving?

Overlay the super six with operational data required as part of your monitoring and reporting.

Need a template?

If you don't have a template or instructions for this, email me tanya@tanyaheaneyvoogt.com with the subject *MAM Please*. I will send you my template for monthly accountability meetings, which includes the Super Six questions and a host of operational questions in editable Word format. You can customise and introduce these immediately.

Chapter Eighteen

The Holy Grail of Workload Management

How do you monitor, measure and manage workload management challenges that range from bored staff members at risk of disengaging to those hooked on the merry-go-round of normalised work overload? And how do you mitigate the risks?

> Workload management is the new black.

Workload management is the new black.

Do not gloss over this topic. It is one of the most prevalent psychosocial risks individuals face in workplaces and one that leaders struggle to address.

In this chapter, I'll give you the answers – and more.

What do we mean by workload?

Workload refers to different factors grouped under the heading of job demands. Specifically, these include the *volume* of work, the *time* provided to complete work tasks, the *intensity* of the tasks (not all tasks are equal) and the *physical, mental and emotional demands* of the work.

It's no exaggeration that most workplace culture surveys are showing evidence of the impact of stress associated with workload.

> **Research indicates that individuals reporting high levels of job demands are 30-35% more likely to develop mental ill-health.**

I am frequently asked to support organisations to respond to distressing survey results. Some are prepared to do the deep work at system level to fully understand and address the risks. My program, Breakthrough, is specifically for individuals who want to get on top of their job demands and reduce the impact on them and their families.

It is a chronic workplace problem. Research indicates that individuals reporting high levels of job demands are 30-35% more likely to develop mental ill-health.[59,60] Unmanageable workload continues to be a leading contributor to work-related stress and employee dissatisfaction.

It's a complex issue that requires understanding the three sticking points of workload management and system-based solutions to ensure consistent monitoring and management. Sometimes, it's as simple as asking your team how they're tracking and them telling you – honestly.

Yet there can be many reasons why your team may not tell you the reality of their world, and you only hear about it via staff surveys.

Let's start with eight reasons why your team members may not feel confident speaking openly about their workload:

1. Low (or no) psychological safety

2. Everyone's struggling with team norms and expectations

3. Concern of burdening others if work is redistributed

4. Past experience – 'We tried that before and it did not go well'

5. Sense of personal failure or inadequacy

6. An organisational mantra that says, 'It's just the way things are around here'

7. The leader is in the same boat and doesn't know how to fix it

8. Individuals don't have enough work to do and fear they will lose their job or hours.

Did number 8 surprise you?

Of the hundreds of people who have participated in my workload management training workshops, around 17% of each group anonymously report that they are under-utilised.

> There can be many reasons why your team may not tell you the reality of their world, and you only hear about it via staff surveys.

Being bored and unstimulated at work impacts mental wellbeing, engagement and commitment.

Overworked employees may think they'd love a chance to be underutilised, but it's a pretty demoralising place to be. Can you imagine the interpersonal risk associated with telling your boss you don't have enough work to do? That's why we need to make it easier for people to talk about or rate their level of work utilisation.

> Leaders often tell me they struggle to know if an individual has too much work or not.

What systems do you have in place for routinely, consistently and safely monitoring and managing workload in your workplace?

Leaders often tell me they struggle to know if an individual has too much work or not. Later in this chapter (in the monitor, measure and manage section), I'll introduce you to an evidence-backed workload utilisation assessment. You'll need to do some work to introduce this and to avoid any fear that may arise and I can guide you through that if you need support.

For now, let's look at one of the most important rules for modern leaders in a high-demand work environment, and the three sticking points of workload management.

Subtract before you add

Leaders in the modern world of work need to adopt a subtraction mindset over an additive one. Subtract before you add: that's the Golden Rule. It's simple mathematics.

In cookie jar parlance, if the jar is full, you have to take a cookie out before you can put another one in. Right? You could try just pushing them all down to stuff more in, but the quality of the cookies will be compromised or the jar might crack.

Subtract before you add: that's the Golden Rule.

Adding work tasks to the team is like a cookie jar. You can't just keep stuffing them in. If the team is full, it's full. You'll need to remove some cookies that aren't as important if you want to fit in the fancy grande-size macadamia and white chocolate chip.

We have to get smarter at this. Be intentional. We cannot just expect people to keep doing more. The data is clear that this is not working well for us – or our people.

We also know that if you ask your team to do more, some who really can't will still say yes. I'll unpack why that happens in the Three Sticking Points.

You must always be on the lookout for what you can subtract (remove, pause, reallocate or outsource) before adding more. That is, if you like your cookies in good order and your jar crack-free.

Where to look for subtractions

While watching the last television season of *The Crown* (before I deployed WDEP) I was particularly drawn to a word uttered by one of the characters – so much so that I paused and went Googling. The word was *anachronistic*.

According to online dictionary sources, it is an adjective that means *belonging to a period other than that being portrayed. Belonging or appropriate to an earlier period, especially so as to seem conspicuously old-fashioned.*

In my work, I help people remove outdated systems, practices and behaviours that no longer serve them, or have no place in the modern workplace. So, this word, anachronistic, resonated very strongly for me.

So much of what we do in the workplace is because 'it has always been done that way'.

What would happen if we did it another way?

> Cast your eye about for any anachronistic tasks that could be subtracted.

Cast your eye about for any anachronistic tasks that could be subtracted or, at the very least, improved to create room in your team cookie jar.

Scan for R.O.T.

Another way to create space is to work systematically with your team to scan for R.O.T. It's an acronym of tech origin that stands for *redundant, obsolete, or trivial.*

Organisational anthropologist Timothy R Clark says it's important to look for R.O.T. as 'everything we do eventually becomes obsolete. ...sources of R.O.T. represent the low-hanging fruit of a status quo that needs to be dismantled'. [61]

In other words, find new, better and more effective ways to do things by making it safe to raise new ideas and challenge how things have always been done. This will foster psychological safety within your team and mitigate work overload. Scanning for R.O.T. can identify outdated workflows, patterns or habits. Eradicating these creates efficiencies and claws back much-needed time to breathe.

How do you start? Openly encourage your team to scan for R.O.T. Hold a creative brainstorming session and invite their ideas about what may be redundant, obsolete or trivial.

> Find new, better and more effective ways to do things by making it safe to raise new ideas and challenge how things have always been done.

This activity creates new energy. Have fun with it, give in to it and change how you do things to create different outcomes.

Remember that individuals can hold deep emotional attachments to their ideas or processes. So, if someone votes for one to be killed off, you'll need to manage it appropriately. Set some ground rules to help smooth the way.

Step through the R.O.T.

Here's a guide to scanning for R.O.T. with your team. This process nurtures those who are emotionally attached to some of those crumbly old cookies.

Step 1: The Why

Prepare your team by sharing the concept of R.O.T.

Plant the idea that redundant, obsolete or trivial tasks have no place in a world of work that is constantly changing and full of demands.

Be open, use inviting language, and be clear that you want them to challenge the status quo by actively identifying areas of their work, the teamwork/function or workplace processes that may be R.O.T.-ing.

Acknowledge that some people may feel uncomfortable if it is a 'thing' they created and hold emotional ownership of. Reassure that the process holds neither criticism nor blame because the 'thing' was relevant and needed at the time it was created.

Recognise that, as things change, the team should always look for ways to make the workload manageable. Release emotional attachment and focus on the intellectual benefits of eradicating the 'thing'. This won't be easy for some.

Encourage people to be creative and have fun with the process

Loosen things up a little. Brainstorming is more about quantity over quality of ideas, so be prepared for some interesting ones. You are looking for innovation. Make it safe and ensure anyone who brings an idea has their vulnerability rewarded, not punished. If there are tensions within your group, perhaps set some ground rules first.

Use helpful metaphors to help people visualise the WHY

Remember the cookie jar? My favourite metaphor is that the aim is to remove those stale, crumbly cookies to make room for the more enticing ones.

Essentially, it's about reducing unnecessary tasks to ensure a focused and manageable workload for each person and the team or make room for 'new work'. The time of trying to stuff all the cookies into the jar without conscious thought is over.

> The time of trying to stuff all the cookies into the jar without conscious thought is over.

If you prefer a less creative explanation, it's about working smarter not harder.

Step 2: The How

Gather ideas and identify patterns

You could hold a brainstorming session with the team at a designated time or encourage team members to do this fluidly in their own time using a shared drive or workspace to collect ideas. Experiment. Ask the team how they want to run it. Try different ways. It doesn't matter if it doesn't quite work at first. Keep trying and learn from each attempt.

Put the ideas on Post-it notes on the wall, or use Miro or Trello if you're still virtual.

Find the ideas that will have the greatest impact with the least effort.

Theme them if you can. Do certain patterns and areas come up often? Or particular processes or functions of the team?

Vote on the ideas. Ask each team member to dot the top three ideas they want to focus on. Emphasise impact versus effort. Hold a blind vote on the ideas if that would encourage more openness. Use a software poll tool or Miro for voting.

What do we mean by impact versus effort?

Find the ideas that will have the greatest impact with the least effort.

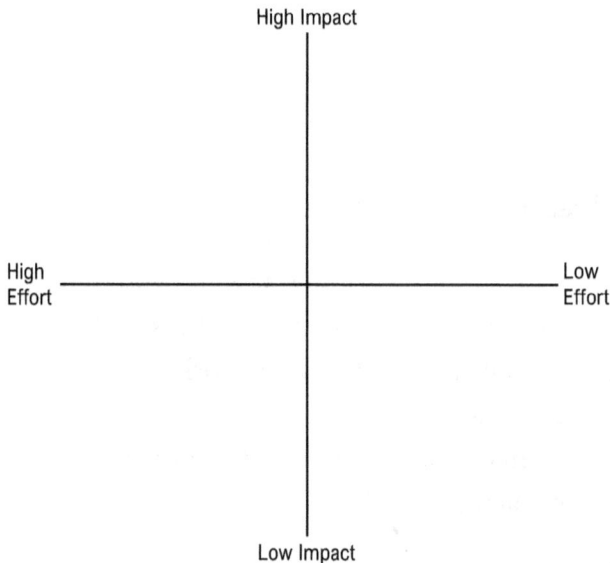

Figure 10: Impact vs effort

Make a longer-term plan to address the areas that are high impact and high effort. Stay with the quick wins at first.

Watch for triggers

I've mentioned some of these already, but they bear repeating.

People may be hesitant to bring up ideas, particularly if there have been fear-based leadership patterns in the past or if there are lower levels of psychological safety within the team.

Remember that people are emotionally attached to the 'things' they create. So, they may resist the idea that their 'thing' is to be lost. Create contributor safety by going first, sharing something you devised that you believe is now R.O.T. Modelling this – even if it hurts your pride a little – gives others the confidence to let go.

> Remember that people are emotionally attached to the 'things' they create.

Keep reiterating that this is not about blame or fault finding. It is about constructively looking for ways to reduce the unnecessary to ensure everyone's load is manageable and focused.

If your team is not starting from a relatively safe place, you may need to do some additional pre-work to make this a rewarding activity. That could involve undertaking some psychological safety training with the team.

Be mindful of team behaviours that seek to shame, embarrass or humiliate other's ideas. You'll know your team dynamics, so shut that down instantly if it occurs. This is your chance to practise rewarding vulnerability. People take an interpersonal risk by bringing their ideas to the table; if you don't reward it, it may not happen again.

This activity has enormous potential to strengthen your team's psychological safety and innovation and address the common and problematic stress factor of work overload.

It is a high-impact and relatively low-effort activity and I encourage you to experiment with it. If you'd like to chat this through or run a facilitated session, reach out for a chat. If you're unsure about the current level of team psychological safety and want to measure or strengthen it, ask to see how we can do this for you.

Good luck and feel free to email and let me know how the activity went for you.

New ways of working

How many meetings have you walked away from, thinking, *'That was a waste of my time'*?

Our habitual patterns of synchronous working are fueling diary overload, with meetings taking up most of the working week. There is so much unproductive time spent in meetings that perhaps you did not need to attend or could have contributed to in other ways. Some meetings shouldn't have been held in the first place.

We revert to type when we need answers from someone or a group. We just convene another meeting.

In her book *Sync/Async: Making progress easier in the changing world of work,* author and speaker Lynne Cazaly looked at how work gets done – generally synchronously (together at the same time) and virtually or face-to-face.[62]

Our habitual patterns of synchronous working are fueling diary overload.

How is that working out for us?

Cazaly challenges us to consider whether synchronous meetups are essential for every work task. For example, could we work asynchronously (i.e., not at the same time) to progress work?

This approach makes our lives less full of meetings. It enables people to contribute to projects, discussions and thinking at times and in ways that work best for them.

My client Rashita is a great example of this tension.

Rashita is an in-demand medical specialist navigating a high clinical caseload and a role with a national accrediting body. We collaborated on reviewing clinical standards to look at incorporating psychosocial risk management into the criterion.

This was progressive, critical work, yet our calendars caused delays. Meeting times were pushed out as urgent meetings arose at the times we had booked. We risked delaying (or worse, giving up on) this vital work.

After three attempts, I suggested to Rashita that we could progress asynchronously, and she jumped at the chance. That would involve me doing a video explaining my thoughts on adjustments to the criterion and sending her annotated digital copies. (More truthfully, I scanned my hand-written notes on a hard-copy printout – that works better for me!)

I've worked asynchronously in other ways to progress work when diary time was challenging. These included voice messaging on phones, recording a video message using slides and explaining my feedback, using apps such as Marco Polo and shared drive documents that people can add to. Don't underestimate the humble text message either.

> There are many ways to make asynchronous work for us in a digital world.

There are many ways to make asynchronous work for us in a digital world.

Think about where you encounter delays or bottlenecks because of access to the people you want contributions or decisions from. How often could you have established an asynchronous way forward?

Experiment and talk with your team about these different ways to work. See if you can find an opportunity to experiment and free up your diary. Look for the improvements in contributions.

And I do encourage you to get a copy of Lynne Cazaly's book; it's illuminating.

Make meetings mentally manageable

How much room could you create in the jar if half your cookies were only 3/4 size? Perhaps more than half, going by some diaries I've seen.

Let's start with that step. Take a look at your calendar and count how many meetings you have diaried this week.

I'm assuming most, if not all, of those meetings are 60 minutes long. For the sake of this mathematical demonstration, I'll conservatively estimate that you have 12 meetings booked (you may be off the scale to the left or right, but this is just a guide).

Now imagine that each hour-long meeting equals one cookie in the jar.

If you could reduce each of your 12 meetings from 60 to 45 minutes, you could effectively remove three cookies from your jar.

Not everything can be achieved asynchronously, so you will need to have meetings. But think about how to shorten your meetings to give yourself and others a mental break and build white space in your diary ... finally.

Back-to-back meetings are a sign of poor boundaries and unhealthy workplace norms.

You will be fresher and more capable of absorbing discussions and preparing for subsequent meetings. You might even be able to take a bathroom break without sprinting or having people follow you in!

173

Back-to-back meetings are a sign of poor boundaries and unhealthy workplace norms, not importance. They're also a big contributor to the problem of mental overload which most employees are experiencing.

Here's how you can do something radical to boost staff wellbeing.

- ▶ reduce all hour-long meetings to 45 minutes
- ▶ promote a 'no back-to-back meetings' rule in your organisation
- ▶ lead by example (and from the top) on this
- ▶ pop 15-minute 'wellbeing gaps' in your diary and don't allow anyone to overrule them
- ▶ hold firm to these time frames, resisting the urge to override the mental break buffer.

To make this work, get meetings on track quickly and be clear on the purpose of the meeting and what you hope to achieve. Here are some tips for getting the most from your 45 minutes and holding firm to that white space in your diary.

Be clear on what you want to achieve in the meeting: What's the meeting for? Endorsement? Consultation? Brainstorming? Or is it purely a one-way communication activity informing members of progress. Be specific about what you are trying to achieve and communicate it to others at the start.

Give them information ahead of time: Send activity updates out with agenda papers, so you don't need to spend the first quarter hour telling people what's been achieved since the last meeting. And yes, that means people need to actually read the papers – but hey, perhaps they can do that in their spare 15 minutes.

Put things in the parking lot: Grab a sheet of butcher's paper and head it up Parking Lot. Anything important that comes up that is outside the scope of the meeting gets put in the parking lot rather than derailing the discussion and taking up precious time. People will feel heard, and the discussion thread is recorded, but it is left to be dealt with another time.

Extract even more cookies

In the past week, how many meetings did you attend that were not a good use of your time?

Could any of these discussions have been handled offline (asynchronously)? Could the meetings have been even shorter if people arrived on time, were clear on what they were there to achieve, got down to business and left social catchups for outside of the meeting time?

Productivity expert Donna McGeorge believes meetings should be brief. She shows how to do this in her book, *The 25 Minute Meeting*.[63]

Remember the cookie jar? Holding 45-minute meetings reduced your 12, hour-long meetings by three cookies. If you reduced those meetings to 25 minutes, you remove seven. That's a whole lot of subtracting before adding. Maybe you'll even get time to eat a cookie if you intentionally look at where you can create some space.

Pull apart your cookie jar

When facing an extremely high period of demand, a CEO reached out to me for support for herself and the executive team. They needed to deliver on the organisational and regulatory requirements (most of which were non-negotiable) and maintain their psychological wellbeing.

After some appropriate preparatory work, we gathered and whiteboarded the key tasks sitting on everyone's shoulders over the 90-day period of concern. Then we asked the hard question. What *really* was discretionary and what was not?

Balanced leadership requires asking hard questions and sacrificing some of the 'want to haves'.

I coached the group through their internal resistance, their unrelentingly high expectations of themselves and what they wanted to deliver. We offset that with their equivalent desire to avoid burnout – something they already felt perilously close to.

The group decided which items could be shelved, which could be supported through outsourcing or external support, and which could be delegated.

We also discussed home and social demands during this extreme period. Reducing demands outside of work to preserve their energy was equally important. This was balanced with the good we know comes from connecting and socialising – and not wearing ourselves too thin outside of work time.

These weren't easy decisions to make. We worked through this plan over the course of an afternoon. The whiteboard was populated with new ways forward and clarity of priorities and allocated actions.

Over the next few weeks, we met online briefly to report back on the actions and reaffirm the agreements everyone had made.

The result was that the team made it through an extremely intense and demanding period, maintaining their mental wellbeing. They also created new thinking patterns and ways to approach these periods rather than just 'doing the extra hours'. That old norm no longer served them.

> Normal for most executive teams already means 'extra hours'.

Normal for most executive teams already means 'extra hours'. Those cookie jars are jam-packed. Stopping to look at the jar from all angles, examining the cookies and making hard choices about which ones to remove is what safe and effective leaders do.

Sticking points of workload management

I have identified three sticking points that contribute, individually or cumulatively, to job demands. Figure 11 illustrates these and we cover them in-depth in my individual workload management program.

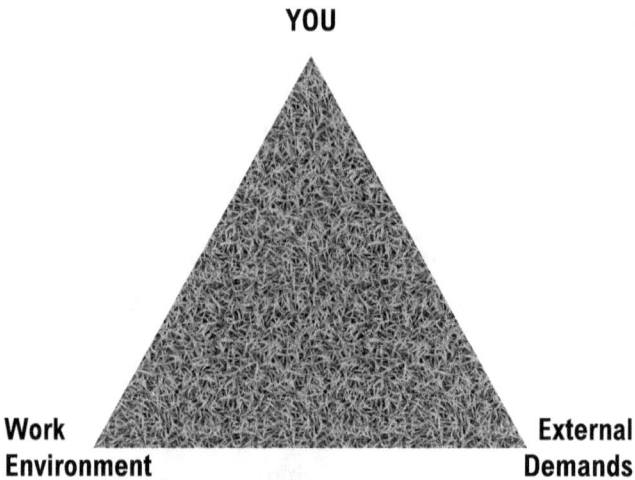

Figure 11: The sticking points of workload management

These sticking points are: You, the work environment and the external demands.

There are often polarising views about where responsibility for workload management lies. Recall the drama triangle in Chapter Two. I see people assume unhealthy relationship dynamics in periods of high workload. In some environments, team members can fall into the victim mindset, believing their leaders and the organisation are unfeeling, unwilling to listen and do not care about their wellbeing.

On occasions, leaders can fall into the persecutor trap and believe team members don't work as hard as they could, exaggerate their work demands and don't manage their time effectively.

What makes this such a complex issue is that many factors are involved – and more than one thing can be true.

An individual may have a workload that is beyond reasonable expectations, but they may also be predisposed to taking on more than they should. They say 'Yes' when they should negotiate longer deadlines or reject unnecessary work. Perfectionism and time management challenges can also be in play.

Workplace culture and unhealthy norms may have unreasonable expectations of working hours for leaders, or set bonus or performance targets that naturally lure high performers and high achievers to overwork to meet them. This is common in the banking sector, where enticing financial bonuses aren't generally achievable without extensive additional hours.

External demands often drive job demands particularly in service-based industries. This is often hard to control or influence, and on occasions hard to predict.

These sticking points are made more problematic when there is low psychological safety in teams or the entire workplace as people don't feel they can be vulnerable and speak up if their work volume is impacting them or they feel unable to manage. They blame themselves rather than understanding the three sticking points and considering what they can control or influence. The external demands – the drivers of work into the organisation – are almost always in play and are the hardest to deal with.

It is reductionist to approach workload challenges through a single lens and likely won't generate the sustainable shifts needed to create more balanced work roles.

It is reductionist to approach workload challenges through a single lens.

Safe and effective leaders appreciate this, yet the challenge of what to do about it remains. As job demands continue to be a prevalent cause of severe work stress, having the tools to address this is essential.

Monitor, measure and manage

The key to balancing work demands is to routinely monitor, measure and manage workload to ensure the work gets done and wellbeing is not compromised. It also means we can ensure people are fully utilised in their roles, contributing to organisational outcomes and their engagement and satisfaction. Simply put, people are well supported and given opportunities to work at their best.

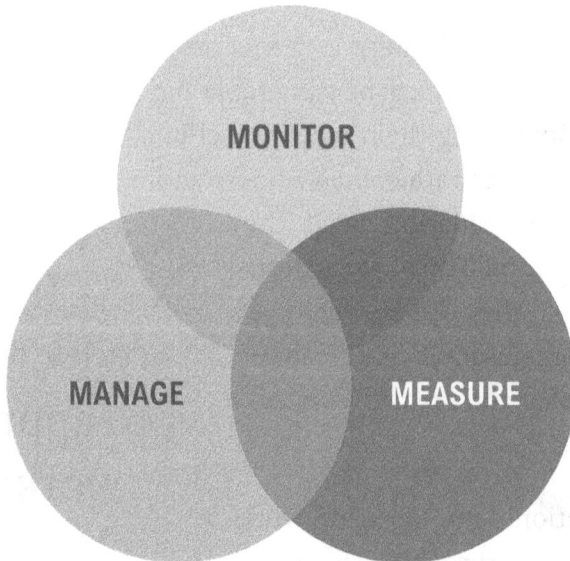

Figure 12: Monitor, measure and manage work demands

Work demands are a recognised psychosocial hazard under Work Health and Safety regulations. A psychosocial hazard is something in the design, management, systems, or application of work that *may* increase the risk of work-related stress.

Work demands include the volume of work, timelines to complete required tasks and the type, intensity, mental, emotional and physical demands of the activities.

Alongside the key elements of monitoring work, measuring work utilisation and managing concerns, I've added some useful diagnostics in the next sections to help you assess and support various situations.

Monitor

Monitoring workload involves checking in with incumbents about their job requirements, understanding that job requirements and tasks can change over time, and being clear on the reasonable hours of work that the job functions require.

Do this regularly through routine check-ins with your team members.

All roles have inherent requirements and expectations which must be met. Aside from the informal corridor and water-cooler catchups, there are two effective ways to monitor workload.

Routine 1:1 check-ins

These should be private, scheduled at least monthly, and consistent across team members. Use a consistent template to support this process. As mentioned in Chapter 17, you are welcome to email me for the Super Six template.

Annual reviews

The annual performance review should also provide an opportunity to formally evaluate the position description and components of the role. Make sure it reflects the changing needs and demands of the business and that the duties are realistic for the time allocated to the role. Depending on your organisation, reviews may involve a formal professional review and development program (PRDP) system or a simple template that enables both the role occupant and their leader to share feedback and discuss role components, performance and development goals.

Measure

Measuring work requires leaders to take four steps.

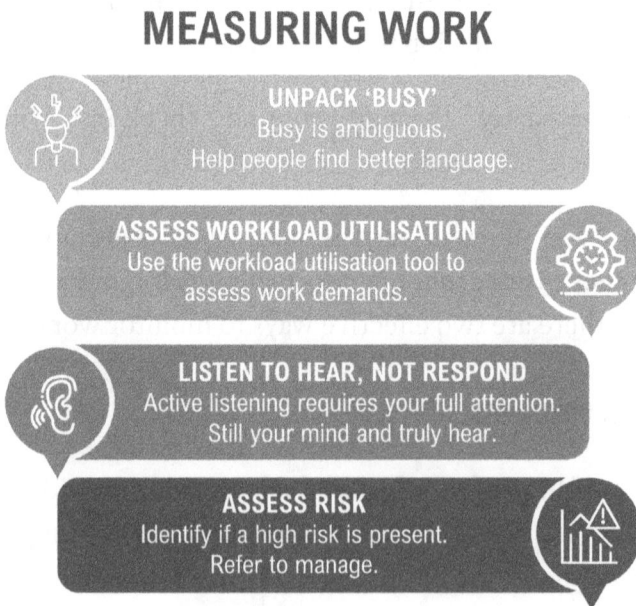

MEASURING WORK

UNPACK 'BUSY'
Busy is ambiguous.
Help people find better language.

ASSESS WORKLOAD UTILISATION
Use the workload utilisation tool to assess work demands.

LISTEN TO HEAR, NOT RESPOND
Active listening requires your full attention.
Still your mind and truly hear.

ASSESS RISK
Identify if a high risk is present.
Refer to manage.

Figure 13: Measuring work

Unpack 'busy' and introduce better language

Traditionally, leaders have only ever heard that a team member is 'busy', which provides no real clarity.

The word can be used to shut down further discussion about taking on other tasks. So what is busy? And how do we know if someone really is busy?

'Busy' means being actively engaged in work, utilised, not at rest. Isn't that the point of our paid roles? We are there for a reason. But because the word is ambiguous, we need new language to measure appropriate workload states.

> 'Busy' means being actively engaged in work, utilised, not at rest.

Assess workload utilisation

The workload utilisation ratings (below) clear the way for new language to talk about work. They provide a framework for open and meaningful conversations to determine accurate levels of work utilisation and assess the risks.

Use this proactively or in response to concerns from a staff member about their workload.

- Green light (deliciously well utilised) – is active. This is what we are aiming for most of the time. This presents low or no risk currently and signifies the individual is engaging in meaningful work with control of job demands.

- **Orange light** (demoralisingly under-utilised) – is low strain/low risk (so strain and risk is present). These are jobs where people don't have enough volume or meaning in their work, or they don't feel valued or see their purpose in the organisation. This is a great opportunity to look for enrichment to retain them in the organisation. While the risk is low, it does not mean there is no risk. The greatest danger here is that staff leave for more meaningful or enriching work.

- **Red light** (distastefully overloaded) – is high strain/high risk. People who state they are in the distastefully overloaded zone and have been in that zone for some time are at high risk of work-related stress. Immediate action is needed.

> Open conversations about workload means listening to hear, not just to respond.

Some roles may predictably move from deliciously well utilised to distastefully overloaded – reporting periods, enrolments, etc. If there is a cadence, plan to alleviate that state during peak times. The longer someone has been overloaded, the higher the risk of work-related stress. Factors that increase the risks include lack of support and an inability to control any aspects of their job role or functions.

Listen to hear, not respond

Open conversations about workload means listening to hear, not just to respond. When you do respond, be constructive. Here are some examples of responses (Figure 14) to workload concerns that show you how to be supportive.

SUPPORTIVE	NOT SO SUPPORTIVE
Let's sit down and have a chat about this.	We're all busy, it just needs to be done.
What are you working on that you feel shouldn't be a priority?	You need to be more proactive!
Let's look at your priorities right now and see if we can reassess these.	You need to work on your time management skills.
Let's have a look at the 3 sticking points and see where we can control or influence things.	No one else is complaining about having too much work.
Any of the above responses!	It's just the way it is around here, accept it or leave.

Figure 14: Choose your response

Assess and address identified risks

If a team member expresses concern about their workload, have an initial conversation and engage them with early support. Use some of the supportive responses in the table above, and make time to discuss their concerns at length to identify solutions. Always stop and listen to truly understand.

Always stop and listen to truly understand.

To prepare for the conversation, take time to assess the risks. Ask the following questions based on their (or your) findings:

- ▶ What is their work utilisation state? (Green, orange or red?)

- ▶ How long have they/you been in this state?

- ▶ Is this state temporary (less than one month), permanent or cyclical?

- ▶ What impact do they report this state is having on their wellbeing?

- ▶ Do you have concerns about their wellbeing or ability to cope?

- ▶ What have you tried so far to reduce the concerns associated with this work utilisation state?

- ▶ What other options can you try?

- ▶ Where else can you get support to guide you further to reduce the risks?

Manage

As a safe and effective leader, managing workload means ensuring any risks identified in the measurement phase are promptly addressed. If a staff member indicates they are under utilised, explore where they could take on enrichment tasks, or support others who may be overloaded.

Similarly, if a team member expresses that their stress from continual work overload is having an impact, you need to take urgent steps to remediate this risk. Seek the support of your HR or health and safety team, or your wellbeing officer if you have one to better understand how to support the immediate needs of your team member.

Then look at how you can ensure a more sustainable and healthy workload going forward.

Here's some helpful questions and answers regarding workload management.

'My boss's capacity for work is extraordinary. But she seems to think that's normal and expects us all to function the same way.'

Sound familiar? It's easy to fall into this trap as a leader, and I've certainly been guilty of this in my early career, not realising that my energy and capacity for work weren't the same for everyone.

The reality is that people do have different thresholds and capacities for work. We aren't talking about tolerating loafers or allowing people to bring less than their best; we are describing reasonable expectations and demands on roles and incumbents.

How do you know what's reasonable? Here are some signs that unrealistic expectations may be causing problems for your team:

- ► You constantly feel like people aren't working hard enough or at the level you want them to.

- There's a lack of willing takers when it's time for someone to act up in your role. (Be warned, modelling unrealistic expectations in your role is a surefire way to kill succession planning efforts.)

- Your people are exhausted, working extra hours and still feel they're not doing enough or meeting your expectations.

- Fear is palpable and team members snipe at (and about) each other. That's because if the leader is not happy, they'd rather you focus on their peers than on them. This isn't quite as Machiavellian as it sounds; it's survival mode – normal unconscious human behaviour in the circumstances.

Are you worried this is you? Take a moment and reflect on your career, then consider these questions:

- Have you ever been told your work pace or productivity is impressive?

- Have you noticed that your ability to produce/complete/tolerate work is above your peers?

- Have you been promoted based on your ability to 'get stuff done'?

- Do you work at your best when you're under pressure?

- Do you love the feeling of completing and achieving tasks? (I mean the obsession that fuels you to do more, not just the usual sense of relief.)

- Have you ever had feedback from your team or those around you that your expectations may be unreasonable?

▶ Have you ever had to pull people up on performance because you felt they were not getting enough done?

▶ Do you use work as a distraction?

If you answered yes to any of these, then your expectations could be unrealistic.

While setting stretch goals and targets and driving high performance is healthy and a key part of leadership, permanent unrealistic expectations are less healthy and may not be serving you, your team or the organisation well.

'I'm struggling with my workload. When I raised concerns with my line manager, they said, "That's just the job. We're all busy." What can I do?'

There's often a waterfall effect regarding workload. While safe and effective leaders need to manage this flow to their team, they may be exposed to it themselves. Perhaps you've tried raising your concerns up the line and have met with resistance. We often think there are no answers, but there are plenty. So, how can you handle the 'we're all busy' response?

▶ Use different language to describe your state of work utilisation. For example, avoid the word 'busy'. It's ambiguous and is often used as a blocker, which can generate defensiveness.

▶ When talking about your workload, be specific about what the problem is. Is it the amount of work? Is it the time needed to do a task? Is it the timelines you are given? Is it delays encountered in carrying out your tasks due to interdependencies with other departments, internal processes or systems?

▶ Are there patterns where the workload increases to an unmanageable level and then returns to manageable? When do these ebbs and flows occur? There's more chance your line manager will take your concerns seriously and work with you to identify a solution if you can be specific about what and when the problem occurs.

▶ Own your truth; it could be the olive branch. Have you said yes too often and made a rod for your back? If you have contributed to the current situation by being too accepting or not speaking up sooner, then say so. For example: *I may have contributed to this by accepting that last project, even though I didn't really have capacity. I have trouble saying no sometimes.'*

Own your truth; it could be the olive branch.

▶ Present a menu. This is one of my favourite strategies in life! Jonah Berger, author and professor at the University of Pennsylvania, suggests presenting a menu rather than telling people what to do, as it offers a sense of control.[64] In workload discussions, try explaining your challenges in this way. For example, *'I could complete X or Y by the deadline. Which would be your preference?'* Or, *'I could complete X and Y by the deadline if ABC is put on hold or delegated.'* A menu means you're not saying no. Explore how you could craft your particular problem into a menu.

'I have one team member who keeps telling me they're bored. They still have plenty on their plate and I don't want to give them anything more as I'm worried I'll overload them. What can I do?'

This is the orange light scenario. Too little work or a lack of stimulating, engaging work can impact individual morale and wellbeing. It's not as high risk as those with high work demands but it's a pretty demotivating state.

As mentioned earlier, the ideal state of work utilisation is 'active'. That means we have sufficient volume, work that stimulates us, challenges us (within our capabilities) and enables us to learn and grow.

Connect purpose to roles.

Everyone needs to feel they make a difference by way of their efforts at work.

How can you put a pep in their step?

- ▶ Ask if they would like to take on a stretch task or challenge. Ask them to identify an area of interest, a project or other work task. They may have strength areas they are not currently getting a chance to utilise.

- ▶ Find a way to connect their work role to the broader purpose and meaning of the organisation. We often forget to join the dots so they can see how their role contributes to the organisation's success.

- ▶ Connect purpose to roles. This is an underused strategy for boosting role satisfaction.

'I have a staff member who keeps telling me they're too busy, but I'm concerned they're just not doing enough. How do I respond?'

Yes, it's tricky. Individuals have varying levels of motivation, which can be affected by all manner of things in the workplace and their workplace relationships. However, they still need to perform the inherent requirements of the job.

Start by checking your expectations of your own work pace and capability. Are you rating your team members against that rather than an appropriate and reasonable workload?

For instance, people have different intrinsic capabilities, motivations and desires for work. Some people run at 120%, others don't. Some are self-motivated, while others require external factors such as a sense of purpose or achievement in their role, their leader, the customers they serve or the rewards and recognition that work provides.

Reflect on the individual and explore the factors influencing their current state. Talk them through the workload utilisation levels, explaining that the active (deliciously well-utilised) state means being stretched and actively occupied. You may need to clarify stretch, stress and strain (as identified in Chapter 11) and the benefits of stretch tasks.

'My employee is busy, but they're not working on the right things. How do I respond?'

Providing role clarity is part of being a safe and effective leader. Holding regular 1:1 meetings with staff will ensure their priorities are clear. Monitor where they may be spending time on tasks that are not important or the current priority.

'My employee is obviously busy but not productive. I'm concerned about their ability to manage their time and focus.'

Regular 1:1 meetings enable open and honest conversations about where you think their time should be spent. The coaching questions in Chapter 14 can help you explore where people spend their time.

Part Four

Getting the Work Done

You're a busy leader with an ambitious remit. Internal and external stakeholders, customers, clients, boards, funding bodies and government departments expect you and your team to deliver the outcomes you promised.

But individuals are variable and modern workplaces have an added focus on ensuring employee wellbeing.

So, how can you get the best outcomes and output from your team members without compromising their psychological wellbeing? And more than that, how can you maximise their wellbeing to ensure these outcomes are achieved?

Leaders need simplicity and effectiveness. They want to know that their efforts will bring a positive outcome. They want material in plain language based on a robust research platform with an easy roadmap for implementation.

Part Four explores models of motivation, what engagement really means, and how ensuring psychological health and safety is about performance as well as regulatory compliance.

There are many moving parts to the human psyche. Understanding the basics of motivation can equip you with key skills, knowledge and confidence to have some meaningful conversations with team members. Especially those you may feel have lost some of their motivation or whom you need to dislodge from the risky stagnater quadrant.

That's why the chapters in Part Four address these challenges through my PEMS model.

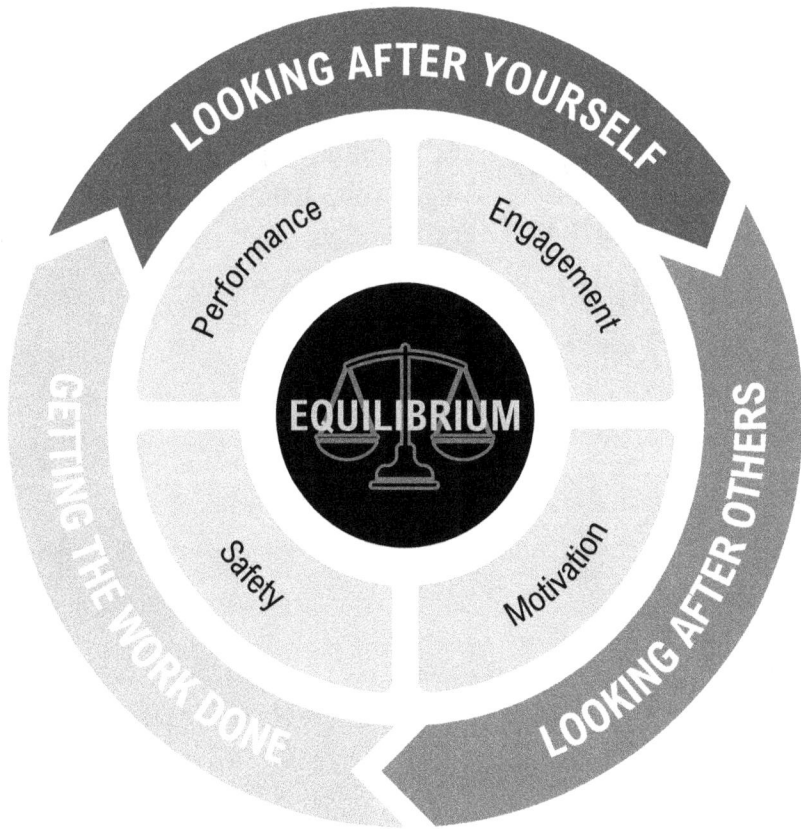

PEMS is an acronym for Performance, Engagement, Motivation and Safety that represents the inner circle of the Finding Equilibrium model. Each element applies as much to you personally as it does to your team. When integrated, they ensure you can look after yourself, look after your team and get the work done.

Two golden threads span the PEMS elements – role clarity and leadership support.

Two golden threads span the PEMS elements.

It is your roadmap to building high performance and high psychological capital.

In the simplest terms, PEMS and the golden threads are your path to equilibrium. It is your roadmap to building high performance and high psychological capital (see Chapter 20) and creating engaging work that stimulates and retains human capital.

Chapter Nineteen

Performance

Since the 1960s, researchers have drawn on a popular model of individual behaviour and performance known as the MARS model to help leaders and managers grapple with the age-old question, '*Why aren't they performing?*'

Recognising the extent of the answer, the MARS model suggested four factors that influence individual performance. These are Motivation, Ability, Role perception and Situational factors. Preceding these are individual characteristics (personalities, strengths, attitudes and beliefs), as well as individual drives, emotions and needs.

With so many moving parts, perhaps you now understand why individual behaviour has flummoxed you.

In developing the PEMS model, I have drawn on the MARS model as well as extensive research and review of evidence-based frameworks, contemporary research on job stress and burnout prevention, regulatory guidelines, employee engagement, motivation, work design, strengths-based practice, positive psychology, social psychology, high performance research and leadership theory and practice. All of that – as well as my own and others' extensive knowledge and experience in supporting high performance and wellbeing.

Drive, emotions and needs

Social scientists agree that drive is hardwired into human beings.

> Drive is hardwired into human beings.

Yet this seems implausible. I mean, if drive is the same for everyone, why do some people strive more and achieve more?

Individual differences occur because drive is influenced by our emotions, which are generated from all our experiences (positive, negative and traumatic), insights from these experiences, and our personalities. All of these ingredients generate our perceived needs.

As Maslow's Hierarchy of Needs describes, some needs are about survival – water, food and shelter.[65] In a modern world, we may need money to obtain these, hence our practical need for work. Higher order needs, such as connection, achievement and power, take us further up Maslow's hierarchy.

However we determine them, individual needs drive us. So leaders might tell a story of a team member just showing up and doing the least work to get through the day, but that person's need for work may purely be about the money.

Others may be there for connection, achievement or self-actualisation. They could even be there for power – which is not as

Machiavellian as it sounds as long as the power is used for positive influence. It's why some people strive for leadership positions.

What can a safe and effective leader do with this knowledge? If you're looking to create a high performing team, find out their individual needs and help them achieve them. Align personal needs and goals with the team and organisational goals for the outcomes you all seek.

Ask questions, such as:

- ► What motivates you to come to work each day?
- ► Why this particular job?
- ► What impacts your motivation? (situational factors, relationship conflicts, lack of meaningful work)
- ► Where do your personal goals align with those of the team and the organisation?
- ► How can we help you achieve those?

Chapter Twenty

Psychological Capital

Psychological capital (PsyCap) is an individual's positive psychological state of development and offers a more comprehensive explanation of what enables us to be psychologically high performing. Four internal resources comprise psychological capital – Hope, Efficacy, Resilience and Optimism. They are often referred to as the HERO model.

Understanding the model shows how workplace situational factors can impact psychological wellbeing.

For example, in an organisation with poor systems, poor relationships that prevent goal progression or toxic cultures with sabotaging behaviours, your *hope* of achieving a work goal may be compromised.

> Situational factors can compromise your ability to do your job, even when you know you are capable.

Your self-*efficacy* may be similarly dented. Believing in your ability is one thing. Holding that belief in particular situations or environments can be difficult. Situational factors can compromise your ability to do your job, even when you know you are capable.

Your confidence and *resilience* can take a knock when given tasks outside your skillset or a challenging task without support.

Resilience is an over-generalised term that is often misused. When leaders are told they *'just need to be more resilient'*, it's usually a euphemism for putting up with severe, prolonged work stressors. But that's not what resilience really means.

Sure, there are some situations where people need to build their resilience. You might well have encountered individuals significantly impacted by events that the 'reasonable person' test would confirm as trivial. Or those people we protected because we were concerned about how they would react to things that others laughed off.

> **Responding to challenges and performing in the work environment is more complex than just becoming more resilient.**

Others can be too resilient if they've strengthened their resolve so strongly that they no longer tap into their feelings and operate in a superficial emotional zone. That's not great for meaningful relationships and living a full life.

We can better understand the concept of resilience when we look at the construct of psychological capital.

The final resource of the HERO model is *optimism*, which is more of a personality trait. Some people are inclined to look at things optimistically, while others see the glass half empty. Background and experiences (for example, a history of trauma) can influence this.

Responding to challenges and performing in the modern work environment is more complex than just becoming more resilient.

That's where the PEMS model comes in, as I believe a person's performance is a direct output of their engagement, motivation and safety. When you understand what's required to generate engagement, motivation and safety, then getting the work done should be a natural by-product.

There's a caveat, of course. People are unpredictable. For many reasons, your team members may not wish to share what motivates them, so you may never understand their innate drivers and needs to help align them to organisational goals.

These techniques won't work for everyone, and when their performance is not up to scratch and you have tried all possible remedies, you will have to step into that hard space. That's because safe and effective leaders don't shy away from performance conversations; they know how to deliver these well.

Every workplace exists for a reason, and in every workplace, we need to get the work done.

Chapter Twenty-One

Engagement

Employee engagement is a key indicator of a healthy and thriving workplace. It's where employees feel valued, involved and connected to their roles and the company.

Culture Amp, an Australian employee engagement and culture specialist company, defines employee engagement as a measure that *shows how committed and connected your employees are. It directly reflects the actions exhibited by your organisation.*[66]

Gallup says employee engagement *helps measure and manage employees' perspectives on the crucial* elements of your workplace culture.[67]

According to Quantum Workplace, a US human resources technology company, '*engaged employees typically display a high degree of commitment, are more productive, and contribute positively to the company culture. They're not just working for a paycheck or the next promotion but are genuinely interested in their work and motivated*

> Employee engagement is a key indicator of a healthy and thriving workplace.

to contribute to the organization's success.'[68]

It makes sense that highly engaged employees are absolutely essential if we want to get the work done. And that is precisely why we measure and strive for this in most organisations. However, it's worth noting that global data shows that 70% of employee engagement is directly attributable to the leader.[69]

> 70% of employee engagement is directly attributable to the leader.

Organisational measures

Employee engagement is generally measured through surveys such as the Gallup Q12, Culture Amp, government sector surveys and global engagement tools. Gallup introduced the Q12 tool in the late 1990s and has reportedly surveyed more than 35 million employees.[70] It surveys employees against 12 needs managers can meet to improve employee productivity. Using a scale from *strongly disagree* to *strongly agree*, the Q12 asks the following questions.

How satisfied are you with your company as a place to work?

1. I know what is expected of me at work.

2. I have the materials and equipment I need to do my work right.

3. At work, I have the opportunity to do what I do best every day.

4. In the last seven days, I have received recognition or praise for doing good work.

5. My supervisor, or someone at work, seems to care about me as a person.

6. There is someone at work who encourages my development.

7. At work, my opinions seem to count.

8. The mission or purpose of my company makes me feel my job is important.

9. My associates or fellow employees are committed to doing quality work.

10. I have a best friend at work.

11. In the last six months, someone at work has talked to me about my progress.

12. This last year, I have had opportunities at work to learn and grow.

In recent years, Gallup has added four questions in response to the widespread adoption of hybrid and remote work. Now known as the Q12$^+$, the additional questions include:

13. At work, I am treated with respect.

14. My organisation cares about my overall wellbeing.

15. I have received meaningful feedback in the last week.

16. My organisation always delivers on the promise we make to customers.

The individual questions used to measure employee engagement can be characterised into hierarchical needs as Gallup's engagement hierarchy (Figure 15) demonstrates.[71]

Engagement Hierarchy Element	Descriptor
Basic needs	I have clarity about my role. I have the relevant tools, resources and support to do my job.
What do I give? What is my individual contribution?	What I give relates to the support I receive, the opportunities I have to do my best work, aspects of my work and the workplace that may motivate me (meaningful work, purpose), appropriate feedback and recognition.
Do I belong?	I am included. My basic human needs to belong and be included are being met.
How can I grow?	I am provided opportunities to grow through task variety, stretch opportunities and career progression.

Figure 15: Gallup Engagement Hierarchy

If you sense that any of your team members are disengaged, explore which of these elements could re-engage them.

Engagement is integral to my PEMS model because it is so strongly identified as a factor influencing performance. When leaders understand the components, they have greater control and influence over direct reports to improve their engagement.

210

Employee responsibilities

It's worth emphasising that the onus for engaging and motivating employees is not totally on the leader. Individuals must take some responsibility for the energy and mindset they bring to the work environment and seek out opportunities. Known as 'proactivity orientation', those who self-initiate ways to remain engaged for example, through suggesting ways to craft their jobs, are likely to be less stressed.

We control our mindset, our attitude and how we show up. If you are struggling to bring your best, check your alignment to your job, your leader, the organisation and the organisation's purpose. Look for what is lacking.

Engagement is not the same as motivation. Writing for the European engagement firm Effectory, Iulia Bogyo explained the distinction. 'Engagement is a sense of purpose, belonging, and commitment to an organisation, whereas motivation is the willpower and drive to act on those feelings. Employee engagement serves as a foundation for your employees to do their best work, while motivation is the fuel or energy required to actually do it.'[72]

We'll focus on motivation in the next chapter.

In the meantime, consider each of your team members. How do you imagine they would respond to the Gallup Q12+ questions? Are there any gaps? What further needs could you meet to improve employee engagement?

Chapter Twenty-Two

Motivation

Why are some team members at your door with running shoes on, itching to get going, while others need to be cajoled and dragged along by the scruff?

The answer could lie in the principles of motivation.

Motivation is described as 'the forces within a person that affect [their] direction, intensity and persistence of voluntary behaviour.'[73]

This is an enormous subject and can be a little circular. For example, job design, job satisfiers, situational factors and work relationships can all serve to motivate or demotivate along with innate drives, emotions and needs.

> Motivation is described as 'the forces within a person that affect [their] direction, intensity and persistence of voluntary behaviour.'

In this chapter, I'll introduce you to some common motivational theories. But these do not exist in isolation from the other elements we've covered, and you will see the linkages as you progress.

The three elements of motivation

Motivation comprises three distinct elements.

Drive, or direction, is goal-directed. Individuals know what they want to do; they have chosen to achieve a particular goal.

Intensity is the amount of effort a person allocates to achieving the goal. How hard are they prepared to push to succeed?

> Persistence is where things really start to transform.

Persistence is where things really start to transform. This is continued effort over time where motivation is sustained until the goal is achieved.

Persistence in the kitchen

Let me explain the difference with a story from home. My husband (Mr V) was obsessed with our new air fryer and excited to explore baking. He was particularly keen to make an apricot loaf cake he'd admired in a cookbook.

The first time he tried, the cake did not cook evenly on the top. It was a totally lopsided creation.

Not fussed, he tried again. The second attempt was also misshapen and the centre was raw.

Determined, Mr V searched the internet for tips on baking cakes in the air fryer. Sites suggested it is challenging and to start with something simple like a basic sponge cake. But Mr V was determined to perfect the apricot cake.

Chef Google suggested using a tin cover and cooking the cake for longer than usual, so Mr V tried again. It still didn't cook properly.

Undeterred, he visited kitchen equipment retail outlets in search of the perfect cake pan for air fryers. He purchased two different pans and was confident this would solve the problem.

No.

Flummoxed, he talked through the recipe and his method in painstaking detail. I listened, but by this point, my motivation had long since waned!

He described how he used the food processor to mix the ingredients, to which I queried if perhaps that was the problem. Now, let me clear up any misunderstandings. I do not spend much time in the kitchen, as I find the return on my time investment exceedingly poor. But I have made the odd cake or muffin in my time (usually from a box), and I do know that certain recipes tell you to mix ingredients until combined, not beat.

I relayed this to Mr V. He re-read the recipe, and yes, indeed, that was what the recipe said.

Next time (yes, still going), he tried mixing the batter by hand. He went back to the original cake pan (not the two new ones now crowding our cupboard) and covered the top to avoid burning. He cooked the cake for longer and perfecto. Absolutely beautiful. That cake could win a prize!

But honestly, what on earth drives someone to such lengths just to get a cake right? Why do some people try five times when others give up after the first attempt?

The answer? Persistence. Continued effort over time to achieve a goal. (Dogged determination and stubbornness may also apply.)

> Why do some people try five times when others give up after the first attempt.

Intrinsic and extrinsic motivation

Generally, we are motivated intrinsically (internal) or extrinsically (external).

Those high in intrinsic motivation generally do things because they enjoy the task and feel good doing it (whether it's work, gym, trail walking, reading, writing a book or baking a cake). It's what they want to do.

Those who rely on extrinsic sources for motivation often want rewards for their efforts. They are doing it to please someone else or because they have to do so to achieve a goal or survive. They go to work to get paid so they can eat, pay the bills and enjoy life.

Yet even if two people are intrinsically motivated to achieve the same goal, why might one succeed and the other not?

Think about it. Have you ever started a new health regime? Maybe with a friend? You walk together daily and live off lettuce leaves. Eight days later, you're face down in a packet of Tim Tams while they saunter past your house in their best gym gear, still glowing with enthusiasm about how well they're tracking against their goal. Irritating, isn't it? If you're both intrinsically motivated, then why are some goals achievable and others end in the pantry?

Why are some goals achievable and others end in the pantry?

The answer can be found in whether you really want to achieve the goal and whether you believed you could achieve the outcome from the start.

While you may believe individual discipline is why some people don't complete study or are unfit or overweight, might it be that they simply weren't interested enough in achieving that goal?

Perhaps I'd rather read and research for hours each day – not exercise. And if I have limited hours of leisure each day, am I not more inclined to do what motivates and energises me?

Of course, I am. It's human nature to direct our effort at what is important to us at any given time.

That importance can be associated with a need, i.e., get a degree to help with a promotion, ask for a pay rise or save money for a deposit on a house.

We are also more likely to expend the effort if we believe we can achieve the outcome.

That becomes very important when we consider how to motivate our team to complete work tasks including stretch goals or things they may not enjoy doing, or don't believe the reward will justify the effort.

Great expectations

In 1964, Canadian psychologist Victor Vroom developed the Expectancy Theory of Motivation. Vroom proposed that the 'intensity of work effort depends on the perception that an individual's effort will result in a desired outcome'.[74]

So if we don't believe in the outcome (specifically, the reward the outcome will provide) – or believe that we can achieve the outcome (an important difference), our motivation to exert effort may be compromised from the beginning.

Have you ever had a team member who did not want to put in the required effort? Was there a clear and engaging goal at the end of the task? Did that goal matter to them?

What about someone who is reluctant to take on a stretch task for fear they couldn't achieve it?

There are many workplace examples where Vroom's theory helps us to understand where motivation may be lacking in our team members. Exploring these can offer insights to inspire them.

If someone has attempted a goal in the past and not succeeded, it may be harder to motivate them again. It will certainly be harder than for someone who has succeeded.

When they lack belief in their ability to achieve the desired outcome, leader support is essential.

Overcoming difficulties and challenges

I'm a fan of historical fiction. In the novel *The White Queen* by Philippa Gregory, one of the characters describes the wheel of life as always ascending or descending.

This image has stuck with me for two reasons. First, it is a gentle reminder that life is not always sunshine and roses. If you mistakenly believe it is, your elephant will race off at the first sign to the contrary. The second reason is that a wheel means the challenging parts of the normal cycle of life will eventually be replaced by sunshine and roses. That can be hard to absorb when experiencing difficulties and challenges at work (or home for that matter).

Leaders can influence their team members to understand that challenges are normal and can present opportunities for growth with the right support.

Importantly, though, they only present opportunities for growth if they are within our capabilities (even if we don't believe it) and if we have support along the way to encourage and reassure us.

> Challenges are normal.

Make it personal

When have you been motivated to achieve something because you valued the outcome? Think professionally and personally. Intellectually and physically. Was it something for yourself (hit 10kms on the treadmill, lose 5kgs, keep that indoor plant alive)?

Or was it for a collective benefit (build that pergola or renovate the bathroom)?

What was it about the outcome that you valued? Be specific.

Was there ever a moment when you thought the goal might be too difficult?

What were your thoughts and emotions at this time?

What made you push through? Was it grit, determination, stubbornness?

How did you feel when you achieved the outcome?

Note: This is a highly beneficial exercise. Why? Because it stores positive memories in your mental filing system that your rider can use to soothe your elephant when it wants to stampede off in a huff because the path ahead is challenging.

Chapter Twenty-Three

Safety

Work can provide satisfaction and delight in so many ways, from the basic needs of food and shelter to the higher needs of self-actualisation and personal achievement. Beyond money, work provides purpose, goals, friendships and a sense of belonging.

Work should challenge and engage us. It should also keep us physically and psychologically safe. Legislation stipulating this has been on the books for some time in most countries. The focus on psychological health and safety at work has often been harder to establish. The causes are complex, multi-factored and subjective, and risks and injury can be hard to see or validate.

The shifting global focus

The national and global economic impact of poor worker mental health is becoming a global focus as we recognise the significant burden to individuals and organisational outcomes.

Under Australian Work Health and Safety laws, 'health' includes psychological and physical health. In recent years, specific model laws have been established to manage psychosocial hazards in the workplace. Most jurisdictions have established Codes of Practice and regulators are sharpening their focus.

This is consistent with New Zealand's Health and Safety at Work Act 2015 (HSWA). Specifically, the Act requires employers to identify and manage risks to the health and safety of workers, including psychological risks. This can involve assessing and addressing factors such as stress, fatigue, and other psychosocial hazards. In addition to the HSWA, the Health and Safety at Work (General Risk and Workplace Management) Regulations 2016 outline requirements for identifying and managing risks, including psychosocial risks.

In Canada, work health and safety legislation includes provisions for psychological safety. While occupational health and safety laws are primarily regulated at the provincial and territorial levels, these acts often include broad language encompassing physical and psychological well-being. In recent years, there has been an increased focus on workplace mental health, and some jurisdictions have developed guidelines or specific regulations related to managing psychological health and safety. For example, in 2013, the Mental Health Commission of Canada introduced the National Standard of Canada for Psychological Health and Safety in the Workplace.

In the United Kingdom the Health and Safety at Work Act 1974 places a general duty on employers to ensure, as far as is reasonably practicable, the health, safety and welfare at work of their employees. Under this overarching legislation, specific regulations and guidelines address psychological safety and wellbeing at work. For example, the Management of Health and Safety at Work Regulations 1999 requires employers to conduct risk assessments, which include assessing and addressing the risks to employee mental health and wellbeing.

Globally, WHO recognises the importance of workplace psychological health and recommends employers 'implement organisational interventions that directly target working conditions and environments.'[75]

The physical and psychological interconnection

The critical message here is that workers' psychological and physical health are equally important. The two are interconnected. Risks to physical health can impact psychological health.

Consider a worker who is regularly exposed to violence and aggression from customers. You could reasonably expect heightened anticipation at the start of each shift. Over time, this adrenaline response can impact psychological wellbeing.

> Psychological and physical health are equally important.

Or the worker whose physical job demands are greater than their body's ability to endure (for example, back or knee injuries), leaving them worried about losing their livelihood or having to endure chronic pain.

Severe work-related stress can also influence physical health. Evidence strongly suggests that workers experiencing prolonged and severe work stress have an elevated risk of cardiovascular disease. Unhealthy levels of stress are also known to cause other physical manifestations.[76] These may include shortness of breath, chest pains, increased heart rate, excessive sweating, headaches, muscle tension or aches, stomach upset and fatigue. Sound familiar?

Your workplace duty

Under the relevant laws, leaders have a duty of care to monitor and protect workers from psychological harm as far as is reasonably practicable.

Specific laws and codes of practice have been released across most jurisdictions to guide workplaces to better understand work-related stress and its causes and to establish systematic processes to identify, assess and manage.

While People and Culture, Health and Safety, and Wellbeing teams in medium-large organisations will be tasked with establishing these systems, it is not their job to monitor the wellbeing of your teams.

It is yours.

Your leadership role

Leaders have a crucial responsibility to monitor workers' psychological and physical wellbeing.

That does not mean you need to diagnose, treat or counsel. But it does mean checking in regularly as part of your usual leadership duties and taking proactive action if you (or others) have concerns.

When building leaders' confidence in this space, I often ask, 'If you observed one of your team holding their arm, what would you do?' The unanimous response is, 'I'd ask if they were okay and get medical treatment if they needed it.'

Precisely.

Monitoring psychological wellbeing is no different. When conducting your 1:1s and regularly checking in with your team you will notice when people do not seem themselves. They may be withdrawn. They may be unusually unable to regulate their emotions. They may look worried and haggard. They may tell you that they are struggling. There may be increased conflict with their teammates.

That is the power of regular 1:1 conversations. These moments provide an opportunity to identify and respond and, when needed, direct people to relevant support as early as possible. That support includes you if work factors are influencing the impact.

Again, you do not need to be a psychologist any more than you need to be a physiotherapist or ED physician to treat a sore arm. Know the boundaries of your role so you don't become a pseudo-psychologist, problem-solver or ever-present sounding board to a staff member with personal problems.

Know the boundaries of your role.

I know without a doubt that this responsibility adds pressure to already strained leaders. That's why I wrote this book – to provide you with guidance, resources and confidence to support your team and still get the work done.

Your 1:1 check-ins provide lead indicators, giving you greater ability to influence the outcome. Reach out to colleagues and wellbeing leads (if they are present in your organisation) for support if you are uncertain.

There is so much variability in human behaviour and mental wellbeing, which makes it more complex as there is no clear rule book. Only guidance, your intuition and judgement and the confidence to sense check with other trusted parties (considering privacy) will ensure you're on the right path.

The key messages are that you are not in it alone and that you can find middle ground.

What you need to know

Let's talk about psychosocial hazards. They are those elements in the design, implementation and management of work that can cause work-related stress.

Remember that work-related stress is not necessarily a problem in itself (as you discovered in earlier chapters). The problem arises when stress is severe, unmanaged or prolonged.

As a safe and effective leader, your role is to understand the common psychosocial hazards, identify those present in your workplace and your teams and assess the risks.

The risk identification, assessment and control process should be happening as part of your workplace health and safety management processes. At the very least, you should have a template to guide you in this process to ensure all aspects are considered and reported and that appropriate consultation occurs.

That is the best-case scenario, but it may not be your reality for many reasons. Having been a senior leader in a complex, multi-tiered organisation, I know the reality of our role versus the theory of organisational systems and that sometimes there can be gaps. Organisations are complicated, slow-moving beasts and resourcing constraints and constant change can impact best intentions.

So this is what you need to know to enable you to mitigate the psychological impact of work and work interactions.

This is the area you can control and influence – regardless of the presence of systems.

Common psychosocial hazards

A generally accepted list of workplace factors indicates that individuals are at increased risk of work-related stress. These include:

- ► work demands too high or too low
- ► low levels of job control
- ► poor support (emotional, knowledge, tools)
- ► lack of role clarity (responsibilities, priorities)
- ► incivility
- ► poorly managed change
- ► bullying, harassment, discrimination
- ► occupational violence and aggression
- ► low recognition and reward
- ► poor organisational justice
- ► poor working conditions
- ► remote or isolated work
- ► violent or traumatic events.

Psychosocial hazards rarely act in isolation.

Psychosocial hazards rarely act in isolation. They interact and compound to further increase the risks, for example, it's not unusual to see high job demands, combined with poorly managed organisational change and poor relationships. Be sure to assess these collectively and understand the compounding factors.

These are the most common factors I see in working with clients and workplaces across various industries.

- ► unmanageable workload
- ► poor role clarity
- ► high demand/low control over work or events
- ► poor relationships (conflict, team dysfunction, poor leadership, incivility)
- ► bullying, harassment and discrimination
- ► workplace change (including poorly managed change and change fatigue)
- ► occupational violence and aggression.

Which of these are present in your workplace?

Highlight those that individuals in your team may be exposed to. To what degree are each of these individuals exposed? What is the frequency, duration or severity of that exposure?

Have any of these issues been raised during your 1:1s or other informal or formal chats?

What action was taken?

What is one step you can take to explore whether any of the psychosocial hazards above are negatively impacting your team members?

But I don't want to plant the seed

Are you worried about planting concerns in people's heads? I often hear this from leaders when discussing psychological health and safety. They fear that if they start talking about it, a raft of issues will come forth.

So, how can you find middle ground? How can you open up discussions and remove barriers for your team?

Essentially, that's your role.

Some individuals will over-correct, but that should not make you avoid these conversations. If you have concerns about a potential overreaction, prepare ahead to coach them through. And prepare your own emotional response. Tame your elephant before you start.

Practice game theory, where you plot out how you think the moves will go, mapping your responses to direct the conversation. Go back and read the sections on workload management (Chapter 18) and stretch, stress and strain (Chapter 11) so you can confidently redirect any misunderstandings, then listen with sincere intent.

Finding middle ground is your superpower.

This is part of the discomfort of safe and effective leadership. Balance is key. Finding middle ground is your superpower.

Enabling psychological safety and effectiveness

'If you aren't hearing about problems, that doesn't mean they don't exist, especially in our uncertain, complex world. More likely, it means people don't feel safe talking about them.'[77] Amy Edmondson is right. Everyone has problems. Your role is to make it safe for them to tell you about them.

Watch for overcorrections

Psychological safety is an environment where people feel safe to take interpersonal risks – to be vulnerable. Those risks are moments when we speak up, risk failure by stepping out of our comfort zone to try something new, or improve the status quo.

We're vulnerable because most of us engage in what is known as impression management. To understand this, reflect on the first time you met your in-laws or the last job interview you went for.

Were you your true self? Did those people see the same you as your friends would on a night out on the town? Or the same version of you that sprawls on the couch in leisure wear, spooning chocolate ice cream from the tub?

Of course not. On some level, we all fear not being accepted for who we really are. It isn't conscious – chances are you aren't even aware you're doing it.

Have you ever held back from asking questions in a meeting or training session? Perhaps you thought everyone else seemed to understand what was happening so something must be wrong with you! (At least that's what you thought until someone finally spoke up and the whole group breathed a sigh of relief as they were equally confused.)

That's impression management. It holds you back and stops you from taking an interpersonal risk. We avoid these risks in certain social settings because we worry that people will think less of us and we may be embarrassed or humiliated. You may have genuine historical examples of being so, meaning you are even less likely to speak up or ask questions.

What's the risk if people are afraid to speak up.

What's the risk if people are afraid to speak up in your team and your organisation? What if they can't speak out about concerning behaviour? Unethical conduct? A major risk to a project? A safety risk?

And what's the risk to your ability to innovate, to grow and learn if people aren't invited to contribute new ideas and perspectives? Or to experiment, fail and learn?

Stagnation is guaranteed if we are shutting down new contributions and indulging in group think.

Stay in the middle lane

I've been teaching psychological safety to workgroups for years and what's emerged is a misapplication or rather, an overcorrection of the construct.

231

Timothy R Clark's 4 Stages of Psychological Safety framework identifies four safety phases teams must go through. These include inclusion safety, learner safety, contributor safety and challenger safety.[78] The four stages are encompassed by respect and permission, however Clark warns that we risk exploitation or maternalism/paternalism if we over or underplay either of these.

> Establishing a growth environment is anything but comfortable or indulgent.

Essentially, we are cautioned to find the middle lane. Clark's model has been popular because it speaks to inclusion and our human need to belong. It also affirms our need to learn and grow.

In my workshops, I also draw on research from Amy Edmondson, including from her book *The Fearless Organisation: Creating Psychological Safety in the Workplace for Learning, Innovation and Growth.*[79] Edmondson is clear that establishing a growth environment is anything but comfortable or indulgent.

This misapplication of these models is in the belief that psychological safety protects us from uncomfortable moments. But learning, growing, experimenting and failing are anything but comfortable. Psychological safety is not an overprotective or indulgent state where people are not held accountable for their behaviour and its consequences. Being safe to contribute ideas does not mean accepting every idea. Sadly, such misunderstandings are commonplace and I often coach leaders seeking help to find middle ground.

Confirmation bias often arises when talking about psychological safety. This is where we seek and accept only information that confirms our beliefs. Suppose a team member has recently received appropriately delivered feedback that dented their confidence or that they struggled to accept. They then attend a workshop and learn about psychological safety and terms such as 'punished vulnerability'. Some people might use this information to confirm their belief that their psychological safety was compromised. We indulge in confirmation bias if we don't challenge our thinking, get other perspectives, or ensure we are viewing balanced information.

What psychological safety is not

'You compromised my psychological safety, when you held me accountable for my poor performance.'

At the end of a team workshop on psychological safety, the facilitator prompted a small group of participants with a question. The facilitator was trying to engage this group in the content and bring them back on track, as they had been distracted and disruptive throughout the session. The answer to the question was the focus of the three-hour workshop.

The group member called upon to answer the question was defensive and embarrassed and admitted they did not know the answer. Their colleagues saw clearly that the person had not been engaged in the workshop.

Psychological safety is about positive intent.

Later, the participant reported to their supervisor that they felt their psychological safety had been compromised when asked the question. Essentially, they were embarrassed at being caught not participating in the learning activity.

Was that compromising psychological safety? Or not taking responsibility for their behaviour? The latter.

'My right to psychological safety means I can say what I want even if it does not align with human rights principles.'

When I teach within Clark's 4 Stages of Psychological Safety model, we talk about inclusion safety and that every human has a basic need – and right – to belong.[80] During training, we explore exclusive behaviours and junk theories of superiority and promote inclusive behaviours as the core to building psychological safety. We also discuss what it means to be safe to learn. Does one person's right to be included and belong, and contribute their ideas and views, overwrite another's if we are talking about topics such as homosexuality and transgender?

I have seen psychological safety being weaponised in a polarising debate about human rights issues. This was distressing and incredibly divisive for everyone involved.

Psychological safety is about positive intent – to learn, grow, innovate and bring out the best in the team. It never acts as a vehicle for discriminatory actions or hate speech.

'My right to psychological safety means people should not disagree with me or my ideas.'

Challenging ideas and perspectives is key to getting the best ideas and outcomes for the team and organisation. We should all be able to disagree, but doing so takes considerable emotional regulation and skill. Many of us have been raised to be polite and agreeable, and not taught to challenge respectfully.

I constantly work with teams who need to learn how to challenge and be challenged. It is not a comfortable or normal state for most of them. Others, however, relish their role as provocateurs and throw down the gauntlet at any opportunity. Recently, I've been intrigued to note some people describing themselves as provocateurs in their LinkedIn profiles.

How we challenge is critically important. It should always be done with respect and a positive intent to improve an outcome for the person, team or organisation.

Those not raised to challenge ideas or authority are usually deeply uncomfortable with being challenged. We rush into fight or flight mode, which often ends poorly. It is a source of conflict and strife within and between work teams. Having our views challenged can lead to people saying their psychological safety was compromised.

Being challenged is uncomfortable. But delivered appropriately, it should not be unsafe.

At higher levels in an organisation, the ability to challenge robustly and intellectually with respect and positive intent is known as intellectual friction. It is a key driver of innovation and performance.

> Psychological safety doesn't mean agreeing with everything you say.

However, it is complex and high risk, so make sure people have the skills and knowledge to challenge appropriately.

For now, the message is that psychological safety doesn't mean agreeing with everything you say.

'I gave you my suggestions and you didn't accept them.'

High levels of psychological safety mean that diverse contributions should be sought and genuinely considered. Inviting ideas and genuinely being open and curious about the ideas received, without prejudice, makes for contributor safety.

Most people accept that it is impossible to accept every idea, but obvious resentment can surface if a suggestion is rejected. At the end of the day, though, the leader must make the call.

Not accepting an idea does not compromise psychological safety.

It is worth noting that participants in my programs often report that they don't get feedback when they contribute suggestions or ideas. Many agree that providing an idea is not a guarantee it will be taken up, but they do appreciate acknowledgement of their contribution and would value feedback on why it was not adopted to help them refine their ideas in the future.

'My teammate spoke over me in a meeting.'

Building teams high in psychological safety means ensuring everyone has a voice at the table. But team meetings get noisy and ideation gets messy and, with no ill intent, voices can be drowned out.

Mr V and I have a very loud and large blended family. They are clever, fun and passionate individuals who all want to be heard. At times, the auditory carnage at the dinner table has nearly driven me mad (I have a pet hate of people talking over others). The conversations are like crisscrossing infrared security laser beams in the Louvre. It's madness. It's messy. But it's also reality and I've come to accept that. Not like it, just accept it. There's no ill intent and it's generous chaos.

Having your voice go unheard in isolated incidences is not a lack of psychological safety. Those one-off moments of over-enthusiasm are mishaps – it's the messiness of humanity. And while it can bruise your ego or press your buttons, we need to look for patterns. If one person habitually shuts down another, that's a problem that needs to be addressed.

Uncomfortable and unhelpful is not necessarily unsafe

We know that psychological safety as a construct can be misapplied. It can also be confused with psychological health and safety and be a catchphrase if someone feels uncomfortable.

Leaders often tell me they hear 'I felt psychologically unsafe' from people who feel uncomfortable in a work moment due to performance feedback, reasonable work expectations, a stretch task within their capability levels, someone not agreeing with them, or others firming up their boundaries.

If all else is equal, uncomfortable is not unsafe. The exception, of course, relates to predatory behaviour or risk to physical or psychological safety generated by sexually or gendered inappropriate or harassing behaviours. Trusting our instincts is important in keeping us safe from real threats.

Being uncomfortable is part of learning and growing in the workplace. Self-reflection, owning our truth and stretching is essential.

Building teams high in psychological safety is anything but comfortable. It takes knowledge, intention, action and consistency. It's tough work.

> **Being uncomfortable is part of learning and growing.**

Unhelpful behaviours are plentiful in the workplace. We hear it often enough when team members snipe at each other and use phrases such as 'That's not my job'. But these instances are not necessarily psychologically unsafe, they're just unhelpful.

Leaders must understand that there are variances. Overlay these with your knowledge of the individuals involved and the organisational context. Repeated, targeted behaviours or those that constitute human rights violations are beyond unhelpful and uncomfortable and warrant immediate action.

Common contribution killers

I've trained hundreds of people in my psychological safety workshops and collected extensive data on the leader and team behaviours that shut down the contribution of new ideas, solutions or suggestions. While the range of behaviours is vast, the ones that appear the most often in our survey results are shown in Figure 16.

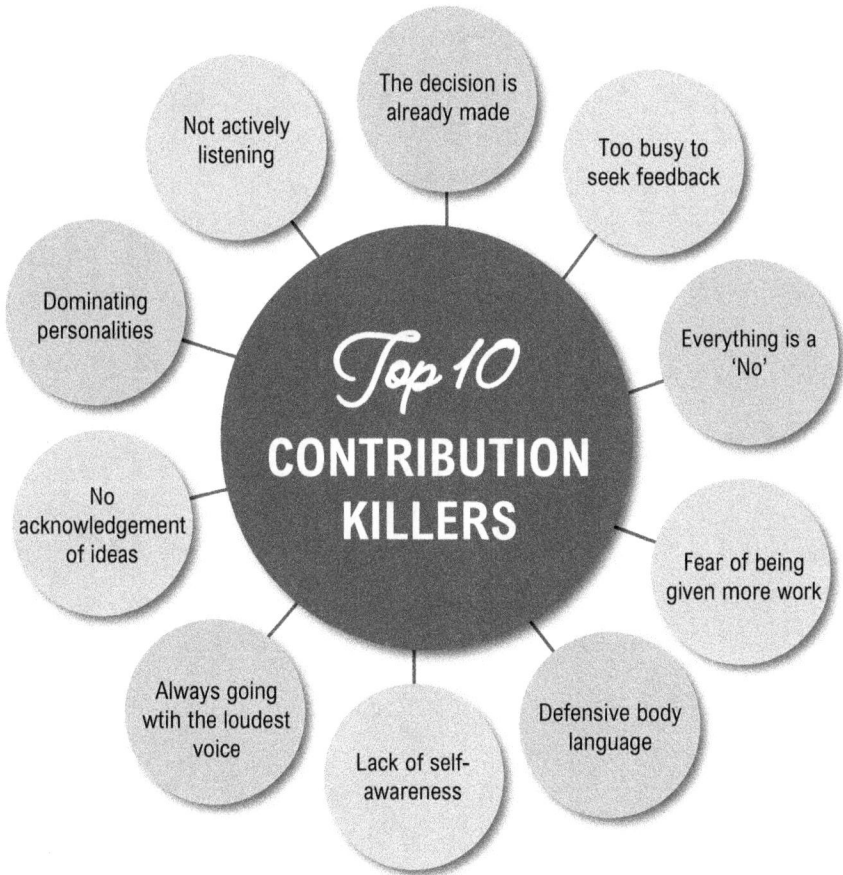

Figure 16: The top 10 contribution killers

Chapter Twenty-Four

The Two Golden Threads

In writing this book, providing safe and effective leaders with simple ways to take action has always been critical. I spent hundreds of hours researching and mapping sources to create the PEMS model. As I did so, two common threads emerged across each area. They are so significant that I call them the golden threads.

The first is role clarity. The second is leader support.

While PEMS is the overarching, easily remembered model, the golden threads tie it all together to help you find equilibrium.

Let's unpack each in detail.

Role clarity

Role amblgulty hampers productivity and wellbeing

How often do you check in with team members to clarify their roles and responsibilities? 'Ah', I hear you say, 'They have their PD, they know what they're supposed to be doing.'

But how current is their PD? What other tasks, activities or responsibilities have they assumed since being appointed against that document?

What else has changed in your workplace since then? Processes? Systems? Delegations? Structures? Other teams and roles?

Nothing stays static in organisations – except, perhaps, PDs.

If you have formal annual appraisals, then hopefully you use that as an opportunity to review and update PDs. But this doesn't always reflect the full gamut of roles and responsibilities you must dynamically clarify for your team members.

Consider recruitment.

When you readvertise a position, do you review the position description line by line, carefully considering the role requirements, responsibilities, tasks and activities? Do you take into account changes in the workplace?

It's quite common (especially given time constraints in modern workplaces) to engage in 'rinse and repeat' recruitment. If anything, the position description may get updated to the new organisational proforma. Urgency to replace a team member often means we miss this vital step in ensuring clarity in the role.

Perhaps we don't fully realise the importance of ensuring the position description truly reflects the job. We'll just sort it out when we get the person. It's fluid. It's an evolving role. All these can be true, particularly when we appoint knowledge workers or subject matter experts. There's an assumption that they know (even better than you) what they will need to do in their role.

But role clarity is more than that.

Role clarity is more than tasks

Role clarity involves far more than clarifying the tasks a worker is expected to complete. It also involves responsibilities, scope, priorities, latitude, boundaries, timelines, authority and decision-making. Figure 17 offers descriptors to clarify a role.

Item	Descriptor
Role responsibilities	What is the specific task list for this role? What activities are involved? What relationships are integral to the success of this role? What targets must they meet? What KPIs? What expectations of performance?
The scope of their role	Can they meet with the CEO to discuss an element of their work or must they go through their supervisor first? What are the professional scope requirements? What is in and out of scope for this role?
Priorities	What are the priorities of the role? What takes precedence? When? How do they establish changing priorities? Given limited time and the intensification of work, effective prioritising is essential. Help your team get clear on what takes precedence through general rules or daily check-ins. This reduces anxiety and ensures that the right work gets done on time.

Item	Descriptor
Latitude	What decision-making latitude do they have?
Boundaries	Who must they report to, check in with, consult and liaise with? When? How?
	Where is there potential for conflict with another role or task or direction?
	Where does their role end and another begin? Task and role conflict often leads to relationship conflict.
Timelines	Knowing when tasks are due helps ensure the right task is worked on at the right time and expectations are met.
	How do you communicate timelines?
	If these change, do you negotiate priorities and determine what takes precedence?
	Are timelines, key reporting dates and project milestones documented and available?
Authority and decision-making	Some roles have delegation of authority statements outlining the parameters of authority and decision-making. If not, be clear on where your incumbent can make decisions for themselves and when your authority (or check in) is required.
	Have you made it clear where they have total accountability to run with and complete duties?
	Do they know when they need to inform you before taking the next step, or who they need to consult with before making certain decisions?

Figure 17: Aspects of role clarity

Clarifying requirements creates efficiencies and reduces anxiety associated with expectations. People don't generally come to work intent on making fools of themselves by not fulfilling their responsibilities.

Lack of clarity of roles and responsibilities is such a prevalent and problematic issue that it is listed as a hazard in psychosocial codes of practice. These codes state the work-related stress risks associated with low role clarity increase when combined with other psychosocial hazards such as high job demands, poorly managed change, poor workplace relationships and lack of leadership support.

> Clarifying requirements creates efficiencies and reduces anxiety.

Signs you need to clarify roles and responsibilities in your team

- ► Balls are dropped. Things aren't getting done.

- ► Tensions are rising and staff blame each other if things don't get done.

- ► More than one person is attempting to complete the same task.

- ► Inefficiencies are evident. No one is clear on task ownership, so there's a lot of double-checking.

- ► Owners of dependent processes or tasks are frustrated with delays or inaccuracies.

- ► Your team member asks you a lot of questions.

- ▶ A team member lacks autonomy and seeks reassurance frequently.

- ▶ The wrong task is being focused on. If priorities are unclear, staff will naturally focus on the tasks they feel comfortable with or believe they can achieve more efficiently.

- ▶ Deadlines are missed.

- ▶ Other department heads complain to you.

- ▶ Policies are breached when actions occur outside of delegated authority.

If any of these sound familiar, it's time to take action.

Steps to ensure role clarity

Make it safe to speak up in your team so people are willing to raise uncertainties with you.

Utilise 1:1s to check in, particularly around timelines and prioritising. This will ensure everyone is clear on expectations.

If there is ambiguity around work priorities, pull team members offline for an hour and map out priorities against a decision-making table. This activity is useful at all levels to identify current pressures and ensure visibility over demands. Another option may be to co-create work plans or 90-day action plans. The goal is to have visibility over the variety and competing demands of work tasks and get alignment on what takes priority.

Respond to failings with curiosity, not contempt. This will course-correct team members who misstep due to a lack of clarity. Reassure them that they can always check in with you to avoid future mishaps.

Review job descriptions and provide more explicit instructions if vagaries are causing problems.

> Respond to failings with curiosity, not contempt.

Develop delegation of authority documentation as needed. This does not have to be financial if there are other blurred lines of decision-making.

Utilise tools like the RACI matrix for shared task completion, project roles and cross-functional deliverables.[81] It's not just for projects.

Manage conflict arising through role tensions by bringing parties together and co-creating a table of task responsibilities.

Leadership support to balance resources and demands

In *Transforming Norm*, I introduced Robert Karasek's Job Demands and Control model.[82] It is one of the most widely studied models of occupational stress.

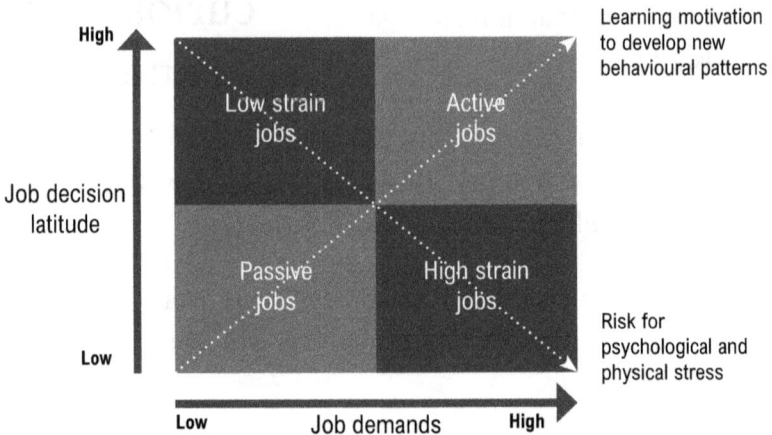

Figure 18: Karasek's Job Demand Control model

Karasek's model showed a higher risk of strain for role incumbents with high demands and low control in their roles. Low control means low autonomy or the ability to influence how or when they complete their tasks. For example, autonomy may involve choosing when you complete certain tasks, how you schedule or structure them, when you take your breaks, or the ability to craft your job.

I still refer to Karasek's model because it is simple and clearly shows the need to address a lack of autonomy to reduce work stress – particularly when demands are high.

However, researchers Bakker and Demerouti have built on Karasek's model over the past 20 years, introducing an element known as 'resources' into the equation in their Job-Demands and Resources (JD-R) model.[83]

To avoid confusion, you will need to park your traditional understanding of the term 'resources' for the remainder of this section.

In the context of the JD-R model, 'resources' means personal and role aspects known to positively impact engagement and motivation. In some cases, these buffer the more intolerable demands of the job.[84] For example, autonomy is a resource, but other identified resources also help employees manage the demands of their roles.

As a leader, your support and encouragement, providing autonomy and flexibility, and empowering your team members to craft their work to maximise job resources positively correlates with work engagement and psychological wellbeing. Essentially, these help reduce the risk of burnout.[85]

All jobs have demands and all jobs have resources. If there are too many or too few of either, the leader can address the balance by suggesting changes or encouraging or supporting the individual to suggest changes.

Employee-initiated changes are powerful and reinforce their autonomy and leader support. This is known as bottom-up job crafting.

Differentiating demands and resources

Here are some common examples of demands and resources.

Demands	Resources
Complexity of work	Autonomy
Role or task ambiguity +/- role conflict	Feedback on task and performance
Work volume or timelines	Communication
Challenging clientele	Social supports, relationships
Misalignment between inherent requirements of the role and incumbent skills and competencies	Opportunities to utilise strengths
Bureaucracy	Opportunities for development
Organisational injustice	Challenging (stretch) tasks
Physical, psychological, emotional demands of the role	Flexibility
Work–home conflict	Skill variety
	Task significance (meaningful work)

Figure 19: Demands and resources

It is worth reaffirming that a lack of work demands also causes strain and demotivates and disengages employees.

Case study

A customer service team was experiencing continued escalated and abusive behaviours from customers. Their leader engaged me to explore ways to help the team manage this new demanding aspect of their roles.

The team had completed strengths-based coaching with me, so they knew their individual and collective team strengths. Relationships were generally good within the team and they spent time outside of work in team development activities to strengthen their bonds. Relationships with their supervisor and their leader were positive and supportive, but their roles were highly structured and left little room for autonomy.

Regular call coaching and a co-located supervisor provided regular feedback on their performance. Communication was good, with regular in-person check-ins and effective software messaging tools that kept the team connected and current. Regular 1:1s sought feedback from team members on concerns or opportunities for improvements. These suggestions were well received by their leaders and generally actioned.

The team articulated that they felt well supported by their supervisor and leader and each other, but the customer demands were challenging.

After a short explanation of work design, the team broke into small groups with creative licence to identify improvements in how they completed their tasks and activities, the relationship aspects of their roles and the more intolerable demands. They were guided and invited to make their ideas innovative and creative (think outside

251

the box) and also realistic and actionable (not suggesting that every workstation had a coffee machine).

I intentionally reduced the time for the ideation activity to avoid over-thinking or refining of ideas. I wanted top of mind, new thinking – and we got it. The groups identified several suggestions to be implemented immediately to reduce the intolerable demands of their roles and improve their job resources. Their ideas were:

1) Formalise a previously informal rule that they could 'take a breather' if the demands were getting to them. (We clarified how precious trust is in this system.)

2) To build their skills (resources), they asked for training on responding effectively to being challenged.

3) To support them during a demanding call, they asked for tip cards to be attached to their computer screens so that during a difficult call, they could refer to steps to de-escalate the caller and when to escalate (forward) the call to their supervisor. This was often the subject of call coaching after the event, but the team was keen to have it as a supportive resource during the difficult calls.

These three brilliant ideas were immediately actionable.

The team felt heard and, more importantly, gained a sense of autonomy in influencing how their work tasks were carried out. Given the relatively structured nature of the role, this was one of the few ways this could be achieved. They had a voice in shaping practices that would help them in their roles. They felt supported and empowered by their leader.

This simple activity took 30 minutes to run and yielded significant results for the team. They increased their job resources and buffered the intolerable demand of challenging clientele.

This doesn't stop the problem. But we know that we can buffer job strain by increasing job resources. When eradicating the issue is impossible, this goes a long way to reducing work stress.

We can buffer job strain by increasing job resources.

Know your team demands and resources

If you and your team are co-located, you can easily observe their demands and resources and make dynamic adjustments to rectify any imbalance.

But what if you have remote teams? Or if you don't have line of sight of your teams every day? Or your teams aren't proactive in sharing the demands they're experiencing?

Once again, we return to the importance of regular 1:1s. Open, trusted conversations with your team members allow them to raise concerns and help you respond constructively.

Take another look at the list of resources in Figure 19. Where can you add resources to buffer any excessive demands they may be experiencing? Together, examine ways to reduce or remove some of the more challenging demands.

Even though researchers have explored this for over a decade, job crafting is relatively new in workplaces. It is bubbling to the surface as workplaces and leaders struggle to find ways to find equilibrium. They must get the work done and maximise everyone's psychological wellbeing, without the luxury of additional staffing or budget or reduction in job demands.

It offers a clever solution to modern workplace challenges and is aligned with the transformational leadership practices that have been proven to achieve the outcomes we all desire – improved productivity, engagement, motivation and safety.

Job crafting (work design) is also a control of choice by regulators for managing the risks associated with high job demands.

Leadership support is essential for finding equilibrium.

The PEMS model and the two golden threads of role clarity and leadership support help focus the efforts of leaders to ensure they work on the activities that bring the best return on investment.

Afterword

Stay in the middle and find your equilibrium

There is a significant risk as psychological health and safety regulations become more known and spoken about. The risk is in over-corrections by the workforce and antipathy by leaders who do not know how to navigate their way forward.

I see these polarising perspectives so often that I wonder if we are losing the ability – not just in workplaces but across the globe – to see the middle ground. It is hard to talk about any topic without invoking extreme views on the opinion spectrum.

Finding equilibrium helps leaders return to the middle. It reassures you that you have a function to perform. It reminds you that those you lead may sometimes be uncomfortable with the measures required to achieve team and organisational outcomes.

Growth, challenge and being held accountable are not always comfortable. But we are not aiming for comfort zones, we are aiming for individual growth and organisational performance.

Organisations exist for a purpose. Our role is to help them fulfil that purpose. Well-meaning, emotionally intelligent leaders struggle to recognise the line between setting and expecting performance targets to be reached and ensuring the psychological wellbeing of their team.

And often, they do so at the expense of their own wellbeing.

Polarising perspectives give rise to comments such as *'You are impacting my mental wellbeing'* or *'That stresses me out'* when appropriately requesting employees to fulfil their obligations. These risk compromising the genuine cases who experience extreme, unmanaged and prolonged work-related stress and whose concerns fall on deaf ears.

Similarly, leadership responses to chronic workload challenges of *'It's just the way it is around here'* or *'You just need to work smarter'* worsen the stress impact and create unsafe environments.

We cannot lose sight of the middle. We must continue to get the work done, look after ourselves and look after others. We must continue to find equilibrium.

If you would like support to do this, here are three ways I can help.

- ► Leadership and Team Coaching – working with leaders and teams to navigate the complexities and intensity of the modern world of work, identify and maximise their strengths and burn bright, not burn out.

- ► Consulting with executive and work teams to understand peak or chronic demands and identify better ways of working. My goal is to reduce common work stressors and high risk psychosocial hazards and ensure the work can get done whilst you continue to psychologically thrive.

- ► Keynotes and training workshops.

Visit my website **tanyaheaneyvoogt.com** for the full range of coaching, consulting and workshop services.

Email me: **tanya@tanyaheaneyvoogt.com**

Let's connect on LinkedIn: **tanyaheaneyvoogt**

About the Author

Tanya Heaney-Voogt is a mentally healthy workplaces specialist, workplace change facilitator and certified leadership coach.

She helps leaders, teams and organisations thrive in the modern world of work through a range of programs and services.

Finding Equilibrium is Tanya's second book. Her first, *Transforming Norm*, was published in 2022.

Tanya lives with her beloved Mr V in regional Victoria where she indulges in her love of greenery (including a ridiculously large indoor plant collection), chatting with native birds and spending time with family and friends.

www.tanyaheaneyvoogt.com

Endnotes

1. Karasek, R. & Theorell, T. (1990). *Healthy Work: Stress, Productivity and the Reconstruction of Working Life*. New York (N.Y.): Basic Books.

2. Walker, H., Maitland, C., Tabbakh, T., Preston, P., Wakefield, M., & Sinclair, C. (2022). Forty years of Slip! Slop! Slap! A call to action on skin cancer prevention for Australia. *Public Health Research & Practice, 32*(1), 31452117. https://doi.org/10.17061/phrp31452117

3. Walker, H., Maitland, C., Tabbakh, T., Preston, P., Wakefield, M., & Sinclair, C. (2022). Forty years of Slip! Slop! Slap! A call to action on skin cancer prevention for Australia. *Public Health Research & Practice*, 32(1), 31452117. https://doi.org/10.17061/phrp31452117

4. Gaskell, E. (1995). *North and South*. London: Penguin Books.

5. Bartlett, K., (Producer) & Percival, B. (Director) (2004). *North and South*. BBC One.

6. Gallup. (2024). *Gallup's 2024 Employee Engagement Strategies Checklist*. Retrieved from Gallup: https://www.gallup.com/workplace/388685/2024-guide-employee-engagement.aspx

7. Gallup. (2023, September 6). *The Manager Squeeze: How the New Workplace Is Testing Team Leaders*. Retrieved from https://www.gallup.com/workplace/510326/manager-squeeze-new-workplace-testing-team-leaders.aspx

8. Rath, T., & Conchie, B. (2008). *Strengths Based Leadership: Great Leaders, Teams, and Why People Follow*. Gallup Press.

9. Salles, W. (Director). (2004). *The Motorcycle Diaries*. [Film].

10. Rath, T., & Conchie, B. (2008). *Strengths Based Leadership: Great Leaders, Teams, and Why People Follow*. Gallup Press.

11. Blake, R. R., & Mouton, J. S. (1994). *The Managerial Grid: Key orientations for achieving production through people*. Houston, Texas: Gulf Pub.Co.

12. Emerald, D. (2015). *The Power of TED* (*The Empowerment Dynamic): 10th Anniversary Edition*. Bainbridge Island, Wa: Polaris Publishing.

13. Karpman, S. (1968). *The New Drama Triangle*. Retrieved from https://karpmandramatriangle.com/pdf/thenewdramatriangles.pdf

14. Emerald, D. (2005). *The Power of TED*: The Empowerment Dynamic*. Bainbridge Island, Wa: Polaris Publishing.

15. Blumenfeld, R. (2018, December 7). *How To Escape The Dreaded Drama Triangle*. Forbes. Retrieved from https://www.forbes.com/sites/remyblumenfeld/2018/12/07/how-to-transform-your-relationships-by-getting-creative/?sh=52f3c7c17565

16. Gallup. (2018). *Clifton Strengths Assessment*. Retrieved from https://store.gallup.com/h/en-au

17. World Health Organization. (2021). *International Classification of Diseases* (11th ed.). Retrieved from https://icd.who.int/en

18. Bakker, A. B., Demerouti, E., & Euwema, M. C. (2005). Job resources buffer the impact of job demands on burnout. *Journal of Occupational Health Psychology*, 10(2), 170–180. https://doi.org/10.1037/1076-8998.10.2.170

19. McGeorge, D. (2019). *The First 2 Hours: make better use of your most valuable time*. Milton, Qld: John Wiley & Sons Australia, Ltd.

20. Parker, S. *The SMART Work Design Model.* The Centre for Transformative Work Design, Future of Work Institute, Curtin University, Australia. Retrieved from https://www.transformativework-design.com

21. Safe Work Australia. (n.d.). *Good Work Design.* Retrieved from https://www.safeworkaustralia.gov.au/safety-topic/managing-health-and-safety/good-work-design

22. Parker, S. *The SMART Work Design Model.* The Centre for Transformative Work Design, Future of Work Institute, Curtin University Australia. Retrieved from https://www.transformativework-design.com

23. Andreassen, C. S., Griffiths, M. D., Pallesen, S., & Sinha, R. (2016). Workaholism: An Overview and Current Status of the Research. *Journal of Behavioral Addictions* https://ncbi.nlm.gov/pmc/articles/PMC4117275/

24. Andreassen C. S. (2014). Workaholism: An overview and current status of the research. *Journal of Behavioral Addictions*, 3(1), 1–11. https://doi.org/10.1556/JBA.2.2013.017.

25. Filimonov, N., (2024). *Why do people become workaholics?* EPAM Anywhere. Retrieved from https://anywhere.epam.com/en/blog/why-do-people-become-workaholics

26. Andreassen, C. S., Griffiths, M. D., Pallesen, S., & Sinha, R. (2016). The Bergen Work Addiction Scale: Psychometric properties of a new measure of work addiction. *Journal of Psychosocial Nursing and Mental Health Services*, 54(5), 48-55. Retrieved from https://doi.org/10.3928/02793695-20160426-01

27. Comcare. (n.d.). *Your Mental Health Responsibilities at Work.* Retrieved from https://www.comcare.gov.au/safe-healthy-work/mentally-healthy-workplaces/mental-health-responsibilities

28. Mental Health First Aid Australia. (2023, November 13). *Adults Supporting Adults*. Retrieved from https://www.mhfa.com.au/our-courses/adults-supporting-adults/

29. Covey, S. R. (1989). *The 7 Habits of Highly Effective People: Powerful lessons in personal change*. London: Simon & Schuster.

30. Thompson, S. and Thompson, N. (2008). *The Critically Reflective Practitioner*. Basingstoke England; New York: Palgrave Macmillan.

31. Balasubramanian V. (2021). *Brain Power*. Proceedings of the National Academy of Sciences of the United States of America, 118(32), e2107022118. https://doi.org/10.1073/pnas.2107022118

32. Wikipedia. (2024). *Etch A Sketch*. Retrieved from https://en.wikipedia.org/wiki/Etch_A_Sketch

33. Mark, G. (2008). *The Cost of Interrupted Work: More speed and stress*. University of California. Retrieved from https://ics.uci.edu/~gmark/chi08-mark.pdf

34. Clarke, T. R. (2020). *The 4 Stages of Psychological Safety: Defining the path to inclusion and innovation*. Oakland, California: Berrett-Koehler.

35. Haidt, J. (2006). *The Happiness Hypothesis: Putting ancient wisdom and philosophy to the test of modern science*. London: Arrow.

36. Edmondson, A.C. (2023). Right Kind of Wrong. Simon & Schuster.

37. Brown, B. (2021). *Atlas of the Heart*. New York: Random House.

38. Brown, B. (2021). Atlas of the Heart. New York: Random House.

39. Clear, J. (2018). Atomic Habits. New York: Penguin Publishing Group.

40. McCreary, D. (2023). *Important considerations for the development of workplace mental ill-health prevention and intervention programs: A white paper.* Retrieved from https://esf.com.au.wp-content/uploads/2020/08/Movember-_exec.-summary-Vet-First-Responder-Mental-Health-Interventions.pdf

41. Safe Work Australia. (2019). *Work-related Psychological Health and Safety: A systematic approach to meeting your duties.* Retrieved from https://www.safeworkaustralia.gov.au/system/files/documents/1911/work-related_psychological_health_and_safety_a_systematic_approach_to_meeting_your_duties.pdf

42. Brown, B. (2021). *Atlas of the Heart.* New York: Random House.

43. World Health Organization. (2023). *Stress.* Retrieved from https://www.who.int/news-room/questions-and-answers/item/stress#:~:text=Stress%20can%20be%20defined%20as,experiences%20stress%20to%20some%20degree.

44. Armstrong, P. (2023). How can HR encourage 'good stress' and limit 'bad stress'? *HRM Online.* Retrieved from https://www.hrmonline.com.au/mental-health/how-can-hr-encourage-good-stress/

45. Armstrong, P. (2023). How can HR encourage 'good stress' and limit 'bad stress'? *HRM Online.* Retrieved from https://www.hrmonline.com.au/mental-health/how-can-hr-encourage-good-stress/

46. Fraser, A. (2020). *Strive.* Milton, Qld: Wiley.

47. Safe Work Australia. (n.d.). *Psychosocial Hazards.* Retrieved from https://www.safeworkaustralia.gov.au/safety-topic/managing-health-and-safety/mental-health/psychosocial-hazards#:~:text=Psychosocial%20hazards%20can%20create%20stress,high%2C%20it%20can%20cause%20harm.

48. Armstrong, P. (2023). How can HR encourage 'good stress' and limit 'bad stress'? *HRM Online*. Retrieved from https://www.hrmonline.com.au/mental-health/how-can-hr-encourage-good-stress/

49. Gallup. (2023). *State of the Global Workplace*. Retrieved from https://www.gallup.com/workplace/349484/state-of-the-global-workplace.aspx

50. Bakker, A. B., & de Vries, J. D. (2021). Job Demands–Resources theory and self-regulation: new explanations and remedies for job burnout. *Anxiety, Stress, & Coping*, 34(1), 1–21. Retrieved from https://doi.org/10.1080/10615806.2020.1797695

51. Clarke, T. R. (2020). *The 4 Stages of Psychological Safety: Defining the Path to Inclusion and Innovation*. Oakland, Ca: Berrett-Koehler Publishers, Inc.

52. Diversity Council of Australia. (2024). *Inclusion At Work Index*. Retrieved from https://www.dca.org.au/inclusion-work-index-hub

53. Cherry, K. (2022). *Fluid Intelligence vs. Crystallized Intelligence*. Verywell Mind. Retrieved from https://www.verywellmind.com/fluid-intelligence-vs-crystallized-intelligence-2795004

54. Porath, C. (2016). *The Hidden Toll of Workplace Incivility*. McKinsey & Company. Retrieved from https://www.mckinsey.com/capabilities/people-and-organizational-performance/our-insights/the-hidden-toll-of-workplace-incivility

55. Myers, D. G., Abell, J., & Sani, F. (2023). *Social Psychology* (3rd ed.). London: McGraw Hill.

56. Gallup. (n.d.). *History of CliftonStrengths*. Retrieved from https://www.gallup.com/cliftonstrengths/en/253754/history-clifton-strengths.aspx#:~:text=Clifton%20invented%20the%20CliftonStrengths%20assessment,but%20who%20they%20can%20become.

57. International Coaching Federation. (n.d.). *About Coaching.* Retrieved from https://coachingfederation.org/about#:~:text=ICF%20defines%20coaching%20as%20partnering,of%20imagination%2C%20productivity%20and%20leadership.

58. Clarke, T. R. (2020). *The 4 Stages of Psychological Safety: Defining the Path to Inclusion and Innovation.* Oakland, California: Berrett-Koehler.

59. Thrive at Work. (n.d.). *Prevent.* Retrieved from https://www.thriveatwork.org.au/framework/prevent/

60. Glozier, N. (2017). *Review of Evidence of Psychosocial Risks for Mental Ill-health in the Workplace.* SafeWork NSW. Retrieved from https://www.safework.nsw.gov.au/__data/assets/pdf_file/0007/360448/SW09005-0518-418530-Review-of-Evidence-of-Psychosocial-Risks-for-Mental-....pdf

61. LeaderFactor. (2023). *Five Behaviors that Foster Challenger Safety.* Retrieved from https://www.leaderfactor.com/notes/5-behaviors-that-foster-challenger-safety

62. Cazaly, L. (2022). *Sync Async: Making progress easier in the changing world of work.* Cazaly Communications.

63. McGeorge, D. (2018). *The 25 minute meeting: Half the time, double the impact.* Milton, Qld: John Wiley & Sons Australia, Ltd.

64. Berger, J. (2020). *The Catalyst: How to Change Anyone's Mind.* New York: Simon & Schuster.

65. McLeod, S. (2024). *Maslow's Hierarchy of Needs.* Simply Psychology. Retrieved from https://www.simplypsychology.org/maslow.html

66. Culture Amp. (2023). *Employee Engagement Guide.* Retrieved from https://www.cultureamp.com/blog/employee-engagement-guide

67. Gallup. (n.d.). *How to Improve Employee Engagement in the Workplace*. Retrieved from https://www.gallup.com/workplace/285674/improve-employee-engagement-workplace.aspx

68. Quantum Workplace. (2017). *What is Employee Engagement?* Retrieved from https://www.quantumworkplace.com/future-of-work/what-is-employee-engagement-definition

69. Clifton, J. (2021). *Gallup finds a silver bullet: Coach me once per week*. Gallup. Retrieved from https://www.gallup.com/workplace/350057/gallup-finds-silver-bullet-coach-once-per-week.aspx

70. Gallup. (n.d.). *Gallup's Q12 Employee Engagement Survey*. Retrieved from https://www.gallup.com/q12/

71. Gallup. (n.d.). *Improve employee engagement in the workplace*. Retrieved from https://www.gallup.com/workplace/285674/improve-employee-engagement-workplace.aspx#ite-357506

72. Bogyo, I. (2023). *Why you should be thinking about engagement and motivation*. Retrieved from https://www.effectory.com/knowledge/why-you-should-be-thinking-about-engagement-and-motivation/

73. McShane, S. L., Olekalns, M., & Travaglione, T. (2010). *Organisational Behaviour on the Pacific Rim*. North Ryde, NSW: McGraw-Hill Australia.

74. McShane, S. L., Olekalns, M., & Travaglione, T. (2010). *Organisational Behaviour on the Pacific Rim*. North Ryde, NSW: McGraw-Hill Australia.

75. World Health Organization. (2022). *Mental Health at Work*. Retrieved from https://www.who.int/news-room/fact-sheets/detail/mental-health-at-work

76. Beyond Blue. Retrieved from https://www.beyondblue.org.au

77. Edmondson, A. C. (2018). *The Fearless Organization: Creating Psychological Safety in the Workplace for Learning, Innovation, and Growth.* Hoboken, New Jersey: John Wiley & Sons.

78. Clarke, T. R. (2020). *The 4 Stages of Psychological Safety: Defining the Path to Inclusion and Innovation.* Oakland, California: Berrett-Koehler.

79. Edmondson, A. C. (2018). *The Fearless Organization: Creating Psychological Safety in the Workplace for Learning, Innovation, and Growth.* Hoboken, New Jersey: John Wiley & Sons.

80. Clarke, T. R. (2020). *The 4 Stages of Psychological Safety: Defining the Path to Inclusion and Innovation.* Oakland, California: Berrett-Koehler.

81. Forbes Advisor. (2022). *RACI chart: Definitions, uses and examples for project managers.* Retrieved from https://www.forbes.com/advisor/business/raci-chart/

82. Karasek, R. A. (1979). Job demands-control model. *Healthy Work: Stress, Productivity, and the Reconstruction of Working Life.* New York: Basic Books.

83. Demerouti, E., Bakker, A. B., Nachreiner, F., & Schaufeli, W. B. (2001). The job demands-resources model of burnout. *The Journal of Applied Psychology, 86*(3), 499–512.

84. Demerouti, E., Bakker, A. B., Nachreiner, F., & Schaufeli, W. B. (2001). The job demands-resources model of burnout. *The Journal of Applied Psychology, 86*(3), 499–512.

85. Bakker, A. B., & de Vries, J. D. (2021). Job Demands-Resources theory and self-regulation: New explanations and remedies for job burnout. *Anxiety, Stress, & Coping, 34*(1), 1-21.